LO-HA-RA-NO

(THE WATER SPRING): MISSIONARY TALES FROM MADAGASCAR

LO-HA-RA-NO

(THE WATER SPRING):
MISSIONARY TALES FROM MADAGASCAR

SECOND EDITION

BY ANTONETTE NILSEN HALVORSON

EDITED BY MICHAEL JAMES HALVORSON

2003

Published by Warren & Howe Publishers
1820 Warren Avenue North
Seattle, WA
98109

ISBN
0-9726655-0-1

Printed in the United States of America

1 2 3 4 5 6 7 8 9 0

Cover design by Robyn Ricks
Cover photo: Peter Halvorson helps process *Kasava* roots in a Malagasy village, c. 1898.
Inset photo: Antonette Halvorson with her children Victor and Paul, c. 1900.

To my sainted parents,
The Rev. and Mrs. Nils Nilsen first missionaries to Madagascar with
the Rev. and Mrs. John Engh of the Norwegian Missionary Society
(1866...1886)

Antonette Nilsen Halvorson

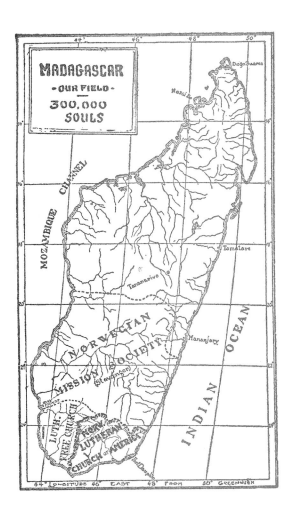

CONTENTS

Foreword to the First Edition, by Antonette Nilsen Halvorson 1

Foreword to the Second Edition, by Michael James Halvorson 3

PART I:
THE MISSIONARY MEMOIR OF
ANTONETTE NILSEN HALVORSON

1 Memories from Childhood Days 17

2 Off to Other Fields of Work 49

3 Called to Madagascar 59

4 Home on Furlough and Return 87

5 Return to America 97

PART II:
REFLECTIONS ON MISSIONARY ACTIVITY IN MADAGASCAR

6 A Brief History of the Madagascar Mission, 1888-1913,
   by Peter C. Halvorson 103

7 A Queen Gave Her Blessing: 100 Years Ago in Madagascar,
   by Conrad Halvorson 123

8 The Legacy of Nilsen and Halvorson Missions in Madagascar,
   by James and Sonja Halvorson 127

9 A Guide to Visiting Madagascar,
   by Peter J. Halvorson 149

Index 157

About the Authors 161

Photo Credits

The majority of the photographs in this book were taken between 1897 and 1916 by Antonette Nilsen Halvorson near Ft. Dauphin, Madagascar. Antonette learned the basics of photography and film developing near Portland, Oregon, after her parents returned from Madagascar and settled in the Pacific Northwest in 1889. She worked in a photography studio and was eventually able to purchase an early box camera and tripod. These tools became invaluable after she married P. C. Halvorson and returned to Madagascar to work as a missionary.

Antonette Halvorson's photography is characterized by an interest in Malagasy flora and fauna, and also in the people of Madagascar, but her main subject is usually P. C. Halvorson and his activity as a Lutheran missionary. Time and again Peter is shown preaching among the Malagasy people, building schools and churches, investigating the people and places of Malagasy traditional religion, or posing with graduates from the school for boys in Ft. Dauphin. Photographs of Antonette herself are rare—she apparently permitted them only during family gatherings, or when images were being taken to mark some other milestone or event.

Many of the photographs in *Loharano (The Water Spring)* were originally glass and wax slides that Antonette and Peter Halvorson used as visual aids when they shared their missionary experiences in churches after they had returned to America. The pictures in the last two essays were taken by Peter J. Halvorson, James Halvorson, and Sonja Halvorson as they visited the Nilsen/Halvorson missionary sites in 1993 and 2000.

Harold Halvorson transferred the original slides to black-and-white film. Michael Halvorson and Robyn Ricks worked to select, digitize, edit, and place the photographs in appropriate sections of the book. The photograph captions were written by Michael Halvorson.

Foreword to the First Edition, by Antonette Nilsen Halvorson

Antonette Nilsen Halvorson (1870-1966).

 MANY OF MY FRIENDS, AS WELL AS MY CHILDREN, HAVE EXPRESSED THE DESIRE THAT I WRITE A BOOK ON MY EXPERIENCES IN MADAGASCAR. This is an easy matter, since I spent my childhood and most of my life on that island off the southeast coast of Africa. My parents left Norway for this field in 1866.

You will also find in this volume many facts about my husband, who worked tirelessly for almost 20 years among the natives on our mission field of Madagascar. He made great sacrifices in behalf of the Malagasy boys, and "Papa" Halvorson (as the boys often called him) has left a living memorial as fruits of his labors. So many of these boys for whom he cared early and late are active workers in the native church. In addition to teaching and personal soul-winning, he directed the men and boys in practical work, as you will find mentioned in these pages. I am sure you will find his comprehensive report in the back of this book informative and interesting.

There is a great need for more missionaries on our mission fields. May this book serve as an inspiration, especially to young people who are planning on becoming missionaries. Truly the fields are "white unto harvest" and "the laborers are few."

Mrs. P. C. Halvorson
Sinai, South Dakota
March 1947

Foreword to the Second Edition, by Michael James Halvorson

Pastor and Mrs. P. C. Halvorson in 1896.

WHEN I WAS A BOY, MY FATHER TOLD ME MANY STORIES ABOUT LIFE IN MADAGASCAR, AND HOW HIS GRANDMOTHER AND GRANDFATHER BRAVED PRIMITIVE CONDITIONS TO BRING THE GOSPEL TO PEOPLE IN A STRANGE NEW LAND THAT WAS SO DIFFERENT FROM HIS FAMILY'S ORIGINAL HOME IN NORWAY AND THEIR NEW HOME IN SOUTH DAKOTA. Some of the tales were dramatic, like the ones about Grandpa Peter Halvorson dodging crocodiles in the murky tributaries of the Indian Ocean near their missionary home in Ft. Dauphin. Others were accounts of more intense spiritual confrontations, like the one involving a shooting contest between Grandpa and a Malagasy *Ombiana*, or "idol priest," which my father told in a way that reminded me of the biblical contests between Moses and the Egyptian Pharaoh in Exodus, or Elijah and the prophets of Baal in I Kings.

But my favorite story was definitely the moral tale that father told us about Peter Halvorson dipping his hand into a livestock water tank to rescue a trapped bee. This story took place back at the family farm near Sinai, South Dakota, apparently when P. C. or "Papa"

3

Halvorson was home on furlough. As my father tells it, one day a bee landed accidentally in the water tank and became ensnared in the warm liquid. The bee struggled mightily, but it quickly became submerged in the water, and the more it struggled, the deeper it sank. Within moments, the soaked and exhausted bee would surely die. Grandpa Halvorson watched the bee for a few seconds; and then, without further delay, he gently reached into the tank with his hand, and using one quick motion, he swept the insect out of the water and into his outstretched palm. Grandpa then blew gently on the bee for several minutes, until the soaked creature was dry and showed signs of life again. Finally, the resuscitated bee flew off—but before leaving it stung Grandpa Halvorson's hand sharply, punishing him by proxy for the threat that the water posed, and perhaps for the shortcomings of its own navigation. I can see my father now, telling this story, and finishing the tale with a little wink that somehow means "do you understand?" My father never met Peter Halvorson (who died in 1937), but Peter told the story to his son Victor, who narrated it again to his son Ken, who passed it on to me. And now I tell this story to my two boys, Henry and Felix, who are just learning how dangerous and fragile bees can be.

I did not fully understand the historic context of the bee story and other curious tales from Madagascar until I read the captivating memoir *Loharano (The Water Spring)*, written by Antonette Nilsen Halvorson (the wife of Peter C. Halvorson) in 1947, and published the following year by Augsburg Publishing House, the publishing arm of the Evangelical Lutheran Church. *Loharano* is a memoir of a Norwegian-American family that braved the challenging conditions of tropical Madagascar to preach the Good News and introduce medical and educational reforms at the end of the 19th century and the first part of the 20th century. The original book is now out of print, but over the years this slim volume has fascinated many readers who were curious about "first contact" stories between European and indigenous peoples, and in particular those who have dedicated their lives to missionary activity and preaching the Christian gospel "to all nations" as Jesus instructed his disciples to do in Matthew Chapter 28. In my family, the extended Halvorson-Nilsen clan, the book has taken on a kind of legendary status—the grandchildren, great-grandchildren,

The P. C. Halvorson family in 1916. Back row: Conrad, Paul, Victor, Frida, Alida. Second row: Pastor Halvorson, Ruth, Mrs. Halvorson. Bottom: Olaf.

and great-great-grandchildren of Peter and Antonette Halvorson continue to read the memoir as a source of humor, inspiration, and intrigue about the old days, and in particular to draw some insight into the family's founding ideals and (it must be noted) some rather odd personality traits. But the surprising number of missionaries, pastors, teachers, and health care professionals in the family today clearly reflects how these values of religion, education, and service have been passed down through the generations. In this way, *Loharano* offers some insight into the creation of a typical Norwegian-American family, and in particular a family with roots in Protestant Christianity and the American Midwest.

This new edition of *Loharano (The Water Spring)* is a substantial revision of the original volume, enlarged to include additional first-hand accounts of missionary life in Madagascar, and information about how missionary families lived and conducted their affairs at the turn of the 20th century. Even after 100 years, most of the narratives seem fresh and exciting, inviting the reader to pursue further studies in the history, culture, religion, and environment of the Malagasy people. In addition, the stories remind us that it is important to document our own family tales, so that they can be enjoyed and puzzled over by future generations. Antonette Halvorson (1870-1966) did not have any special literary gifts that made her an excellent storyteller; she simply had the willingness and the honesty to write down her experiences so that her family and friends could enjoy them. Although she lived in a fascinating time and place, many of us live in fascinating times and places too, especially from the perspective of 100 years distance.

From a modern standpoint, many of the stories in this book may seem dated or even shocking. Life was hard in sub-Saharan Africa in the late 19th century, and modern conveniences that so many of us take for granted today—indoor plumbing, electricity, basic transportation, medicine, regular mail—were simply unavailable. The boat trip from Norway to Madagascar took weeks on a wooden sailing ship, and it was not uncommon for people to die along the way and be buried at sea, as one of the Nilsen children was. Once in Madagascar, the missionaries did their best to adapt to a new way of life and tend to their appointed work, but at least one of the men persisted in his traditional dressing habits, wearing a full Norwegian wool suit for years in the tropical heat, instead of cooler indigenous clothing.

The missionary women were full partners in the work of the Church, but they were also subject to the constraining gender restrictions of 19th-century European life. These restrictions were especially prominent in Norwegian Lutheran communities that were under the influence of late 19th-century pietism, a strain of conservative Protestant religiosity known for devout religious faith, literal interpretation of the Bible, and abstinence from alcohol, dancing, and card playing. This meant that the women continued to wear their formal Norwegian clothing, were charged with the spiritual development of the children, and generally did not participate in the larger political or religious decisions of the family or community. Early photographs of the missionary women in Madagascar occasionally depict them on formal outings with native porters holding sun umbrellas over them, so that their fair white skin would not be damaged by the tropical heat. And on more than one occasion, the

Nilsen children complained that their sewing and handwork projects were torn out by a resolute mother because the children had tried to complete them on the Sabbath, which was to be reserved for rest and religious contemplation.

In addition to these cultural differences that separate us from the 19th century, missionary tales from this time period also bring up uncomfortable contrasts between the white European missionaries who brought Christianity to isolated areas, and the black "natives" or "heathen" who lived there. These tensions are conspicuously explored by Antonette and Peter Halvorson in their memoirs, and the language they use to describe religious interactions and conflicts is both sensitive and occasionally jarring to the modern reader. When discussing the issue of language and ethnic sensitivity with my father, who lived with Antonette for several years, I was told that although Antonette did occasionally use

P. C. Halvorson with a Malagasy family.

the dismissive racial categories of the late 19th century, she was also one of the most loving and accepting people that he has ever met. He said that her love for the Malagasy people, and her love for Christ, were the major factors that motivated her to spend so much of her life working in the mission fields of Madagascar.

Although Antonette was clearly a product of her time and culture (as we all are), she was born in Madagascar and lived there until the age of 16, speaking both the Malagasy dialect of the central highlands and the Norwegian language. When she arrived in Liverpool for the first time in 1887, she commented on how "strange it was to see so many white people together in one place"— a white majority was simply a new concept for her. In other words,

7

Antonette, more than most European missionaries of the 19th century, was a product of both European and Malagasy cultures, and this probably served to reduce her racial prejudice.

Antonette and Peter Halvorson lived in an era that witnessed the final agonizing years of the African slave trade, the American Civil War and Reconstruction, the destructive forces of colonization described by Joseph Conrad (*Heart of Darkness*), and the moving yet ethnically charged writings of Mark Twain (*Huckleberry Finn*). When family members asked me if I planned to remove terms such as "native" and "heathen" from Antonette's memoir, to conform to the more ethnically sensitive language that we value today, I replied that Antonette's memoir is an authentic historic document that gives us rare and important insights into the tensions of language, ethnicity, and culture that accompany all true missionary ventures and "first contact" stories. The actors of the past must speak to us in their own words, so that we can understand how to make sense of them today and comprehend what drove them to accomplish what they did. Contrasts such as these are especially important to under-stand in our modern era of religious plurality and religious indiffer-ence. How, in the end, do religious people share what they believe to be true with other people? How has this work been attempted in the past, and how should it be attempted in the future?

COLONIAL CONTEXT

The missionary work of the Nilsens and Halvorsons fits into the early colonial context of Madagascar, an island that probably gets its name from a corruption of the word Mogadishu, a town on the coast of Somalia that Marco Polo first included in his notes (but did not visit) while returning from his famous visit to China in the 13th century. Humans have lived on Madagascar for about 2,000 years, but the first European to land was the Portuguese sea captain Diego Dias, who was sailing around the Cape of Good Hope on his way to India in the year 1500. After this beginning, it was the English and the French among the Europeans who contested for Madagascar, and in the 17th and 18th centuries both countries established primitive settlements there, as did numerous sea pirates. In the late 18th century, the Merina tribe emerged as the strongest of the 18 indigenous tribes of Madagascar, and established a capital in the central highlands called Antananarivo. The ruler Andrianampoinimerina (literally, "the prince in the heart of Imerina") built an extensive empire based on rice production there, and he also subdued the Betsileo tribe in the south, in an area where Nils Nilsen (the father of Antonette and one of the first Lutheran missionaries to Madagascar) would later begin his mission work. With the help of the English, Andrianampoinimerina's son Radama I unified most of the island in the early 19th century, and in return for their military assistance, Radama opened the country to English missionaries, who built a few churches, wrote down the Malagasy language, translated the Christian Bible into Malagasy, and engaged in limited missionary activity. The English also brought a few technical advances to Madagascar, such as aqueducts and reservoirs, brick manufacturing, and a printing press.

In 1835, the widow and successor to Radama (Ranavalona I) reversed her husband's policy of religious tolerance and outlawed Christianity, putting to death many of the early Malagasy Christians who would not renounce their new faith. In 1849, the queen's forces arrested 2000 Malagasy Christians; 100 of them were flogged and sentenced to life in chains and hard labor, and 18 were killed by burning or being thrown off a ceremonial cliff.[1] In 1861, Queen Ranavalona died and her son Radama II came to power. He immediately reversed his mother's positions and welcomed back the Christian missionaries—this time both the English Protestants and the French Catholics. Although Radama II died after only one year in office, his wife, Rasoherina, continued his policies and established a formal treaty with the English in 1865, which led to the opening up of additional mission fields. A second queen, Ranavalona II, continued this course of action after she took office and converted to Christianity with her court in 1869. Finally, Ranavalona III was coronated in 1883, an event that the young Antonette Nilsen witnessed in Antananarivo. Antonette wrote that "the queen wore a red dress with a long train, trimmed with gold, and— look[ed] sad." The people explained this by the fact that the queen's husband had recently died mysteriously and the queen was now being forced to marry the prime

1. Peter Tyson, *The Eighth Continent: Life, Death, and Discovery in the Lost World of Madagascar* (New York: Perennial, 2000), p. 9.

Malagasy warrior with spear and French flintlock rifle.

minister, who held most of the real power in the government. Despite these intrigues, it was the new series of pro-European rulers and policies that opened up the mission field for the Norwegian Mission Society and the first Lutheran missionaries who traveled to the island in 1866, Nils Nilsen (1834-1923) and Rev. John Engh. Both men would remain in Madagascar for 20 years, along with their families.

Another important aspect of Antonette's memoir is the historical material that describes the beginning of the colonial wars with France in Madagascar (Chapter 3). In 1890, England signed a treaty with France recognizing the French colonial claims to Madagascar as long as the French recognized the parallel claims of the English to Zanzibar, an island off the coast of modern Tanzania in East Africa. After this agreement, the French began a military conquest of Madagascar, which began in December 1894, and was concluded on October 1, 1895, when the French captured the capital city of Antananarivo. Although the French did bring technical advances to Madagascar, the French colonial system was harsh on the Malagasy people, and it was known, in particular, for its ruthless judicial system, which asserted different laws for the French and for the Malagasy. In the first decades of the 20th century, Malagasy rebels known as *Menalamba* ("red cloth") launched a series of revolts protesting this French rule, and the European and American missionaries were often caught in the middle of the conflicts. In 1904, for example, the Halvorsons were forced to flee the mission and the boys' school, make arrangements to hide the Malagasy children they were caring for, and take refuge in nearby Ft. Dauphin. It is in this context that the difficulties and complexities of the colonial system and missionary life in Madagascar should be appreciated and understood. As Antonette writes, "the rebels were planning to rid their country of missionaries, too, as well as the French people—for they [were considered] brethren." Madagascar finally regained its political independence from France on June 26, 1960.

CONTENTS

Loharano (The Water Spring) begins with Antonette Halvorson's memoir of life in the Madagascar mission fields, which she completed at the urging of friends, relatives, and church members in 1947. Her essay includes numerous photographs from the original book she published, and several additional images uncovered recently by family members that were not included in the first edition of *Loharano*. I have also added a few footnotes to the text to explain the historic context of the mission work, to clarify unfamiliar words and terms, and to identify as much as possible the people and places being discussed.

The second part of the book contains a collection of essays about the state of Lutheran missionary activity in central and southern Madagascar after the original Nilsen and Halvorson missions were completed, written by four succeeding generations of Halvorson family members who have visited and worked in Madagascar. In Chapter 6, Pastor Peter C. Halvorson (1866-1937) describes the Madagascar mission field from 1888 to 1913, a period of rapid Christian conversion and development in southern Madagascar. In Chapter 7, Antonette and Peter's son, Pastor Conrad Halvorson (1904-74), describes the state of the Malagasy Lutheran Church at the 100-year anniversary of Lutheran missionary activity in Madagascar. This essay was not included in the original book, but was published by *The Lutheran Standard* in 1967 to acknowledge the founding of the first Lutheran church in Betafo, Madagascar.

In 2000, James Halvorson (1937-), a grandson of Antonette and Peter Halvorson, and his wife, Sonja, visited Madagascar to pick up the trail of the original Nilsen and Halvorson missions and to determine to what extent they had borne fruit and left material remains. In the essay *The Legacy of Nilsen and Halvorson Missions in Madagascar* (Chapter 8), they describe what it is like to visit the original missionary settlements in Betafo, Loharano, and Ft. Dauphin today; how it is to sing, eat, worship, and travel with the Malagasy people; and the extent to which oral histories of the Nilsen and Halvorson families are still a part of

A grove of giant baobab trees (*Adansonia grandidieri*) which the Halvorsons heard the Malagasy call *Zan*. Leafless in winter, the baobab is often called "the upside-down tree." Seven kinds of baobab are native to Madagascar, while all of Africa has only one species.

Malagasy culture. This essay highlights, in particular, the ways that early missionary work has continued to produce fruit in Madagascar, and how exciting and diverse the country of Madagascar really is for people who have an opportunity to visit it. Finally, in Chapter 9, one of Antonette and Peter's great-grandchildren (Dr. Peter J. Halvorson, 1966-) describes what Madagascar was like when he visited the country in 1993 during an intensive period of medical school training. From the younger Peter Halvorson's report, we learn what current medical conditions are like in Madagascar, and we also gain helpful tips for planning our own trips to this unique island country.

It is good to keep Madagascar in our hearts and minds today for environmental and political reasons, as well as for the spiritual considerations that are the primary focus of this book. The island of Madagascar contains such a diversity of plant and animal species that biologists routinely call it a *megadiversity* country, with one of the highest concentrations of the Earth's plants and animals. Of the estimated 10,000 to 12,000 species of vascular plants on the island, more than 80 percent are thought to be endemic to Madagascar; that is, they occur nowhere else in the world.[2] This is true of many animal

2. Ibid., p. xvi.

12

species as well. For example, there are currently 33 species of lemur living on Madagascar, and 100 percent of these fascinating primates are considered endemic to the island. Yet many of the rarest plants and animals are in danger in Madagascar, and the rate of species extinction is projected to continue at an alarming pace. Since the arrival of humans about 2000 years ago, 15 to 17 species of lemur have become extinct. And as Antonette Halvorson recollects in her memoir, the giant elephant bird (*Aepyornis maximus*)—the heaviest bird that ever lived—is also gone forever now, although the Halvorsons found two of its rare and giant eggs preserved in the sand while they were working in Madagascar.

Along with the environmental problems associated with defor-estation, soil erosion, and species extinction, political unrest has recently threatened this important island country and its inhabitants. In February 2002, hundreds of thousands of Malagasy people, includ-ing numerous representatives of the Malagasy Lutheran Church, protested in Antananarivo over the results of a questionable presiden-tial election that took place in December 2001. For several months afterward, the country was torn by political unrest, and the general instability had a ripple effect on Madagascar's economy and interna-tional relations. During a recent short-term mission trip to Tanzania in East Africa (May 2002), I person-ally encountered several American missionary workers and Peace Corps volunteers assigned to Madagascar who had been asked to leave the country for the African mainland due

Female missionary working with a group of Malagasy.

to the political instability in Madagascar. In the same month, a Lutheran missionary to Madagascar reported that in the provinces several people had been killed and blockades were preventing food, medicine, and fuel from reaching different parts of the country.[3] As

3. ELCA missionary Mark Rich, quoted in Elizabeth Hunter, "Peaceful Protest," *The Lutheran* (May 2002), p. 47.

of September 2002, the political crisis seems to have eased, and the newly elected president of Madagascar (Marc Ravalomanana) has been largely recognized by Malagasy citizens and international groups. However, the people and the environment of Madagascar continue to suffer and experience profound need. It is our responsibility to understand this plight and help as we can.

The preparation of a new edition of *Loharano (The Water Spring)* would not have been possible without the generous help and support of numerous people. I would like to thank Ken Morris, Harold Halvorson, and David Halvorson for supplying additional historic photographs of the early Madagascar missions; Ardys Anderson, Linda Halvorson, and Dean Holmes for careful proofreading; and my father, Kenneth C. Halvorson, for our many conversations about Madagascar over the years. James, Sonja, and Peter Halvorson were kind enough to share their experiences about visiting Madagascar with me, and they wrote the fascinating travel essays about Madagascar that you see in this book. Arne Samuelsen, Senior Academic Librarian for the Norwegian Mission Society (Stavanger, Norway), supplied me with useful books and materials that supported the historic content of this work. Philip Nordquist, an historian and colleague of mine at Pacific Lutheran University, taught me much about early Lutheranism in America and the intricacies of Lutheran denominations. In terms of the book's production, Mary Miller typed the manuscript and supplied other useful word processing services. Robyn Ricks, desktop publishing specialist extraordinaire, prepared the book design and finalized the layout of the manuscript; in addition, she helped me to digitize and restore the remaining old photographs as much as possible. Finally, I would like to thank my own immediate family—Kim, Henry, and Felix Halvorson—for their constant love and support. I look forward to reading the stories that you will write.

Michael James Halvorson
Visiting Assistant Professor of History
University of Washington
Seattle, Washington
September 2002

PART I

THE MISSIONARY MEMOIR OF
ANTONETTE NILSEN HALVORSON

CHAPTER I
MEMORIES FROM CHILDHOOD DAYS

Antonette Halvorson at the age of 11 years.

THE ISLAND OF MADAGASCAR IS MY BIRTHPLACE, AND I SHOULD LIKE TO BEGIN THIS ACCOUNT BY GIVING A BRIEF DESCRIPTION OF THAT PART OF THE WORLD.

Madagascar, the third largest island on the earth, lies off the southeastern coast of Africa. It is over 1,000 miles long, and from 300 to 400 miles wide. The climate is tropical—hot practically the year around, especially along the coast. In the interior, where the land rises higher, and up among the lofty mountains, the climate is not so hot. The winter season comes in June and July, and then it is quite chilly up in the highlands, so much so that there is often frost on the ground in the mornings, and now and then pails of water are covered with thin ice, which I well remember.

A dense forest girds the island like a belt and stretches some distance up towards the highlands. In the interior, however, there are comparatively small groves here and there. According to tradition, there were some forests there in days of old, but they are not there now.

A great number of valuable hardwood trees—mahogany, ebony, and others—are found in the forests. There are many large rivers teeming with crocodiles. Crocodiles are rarely seen in the interior, but near the coast where the climate is hot they certainly thrive!

The natives of Madagascar are of the Malay race. Their speech usually sounds very clear and ringing. It is said that there are about 21 tribes in all, and in bygone days each tribe had a petty king. A head king or queen rules over them all, however. There was great enmity among those tribes, and often they were at war with one another. The island is not densely populated. The capital city, Antananarivo (abbreviated to "Tananarive," meaning "a city of thousands"), is located inland.

In the year 1866 the Norwegian Mission Society sent the first missionaries to Madagascar, John Engh and Nils Nilsen. These two young men spent the first year in the capital city, mainly to study the language.

A group of mission friends in Norway arranged to have a three-mast sailship built, in which to bring missionaries to Africa and Madagascar. The ship was named *Elieser*. A year after the first missionaries had arrived, the *Elieser* brought more missionaries to the new field. Among the passengers there were two pioneer missionaries, and there were other brides-to-be, too. They first went to South Africa. Bishop Schreuder accompanied the two ladies to Madagascar. His special errand was to arrange with the government about the beginning of mission work on the island. The two young couples were united in marriage by Bishop Schreuder. That festive event took place in Antananarivo. Mr. and Mrs. Nils Nilsen were my parents.[4]

My parents and the Enghs worked on our mission field in Madagascar for 20 years, after they had spent the first year in Africa

4. Antonette's mother was Inger Omundsdotter Heskestad (1845-1921), a woman from Rogalund County in Norway that apparently met Nils Nilsen (also spelled Nilssen) while he was preparing for missionary work in Stavanger, Norway. Antonette was probably named after her maternal grandmother, Antonette Thorkelsdotter Ulrack—a tradition that Antonette and Peter Halvorson continued when they named their first son Paul Anton Halvorson.

before coming to the field.

When they were able to speak and understand the Malagasy language to some extent, these young missionaries set out on a four-day journey into the interior, southwest of the capital city, to

Antonette Halvorson's parents, Missionary Nils Nilsen and Inger Nilsen. Nilsen, pioneer from Norway, landed in Madagascar August 12, 1866.

a thickly populated district. They had heard of Betafo ("many houseroofs") in the district of the Betsileo tribe. There the Norwegians had their first and largest mission field, which has been independent for many years. The Malagasy are in full charge of the work in the older congregations, are served by Malagasy pastors, and are self-supporting. They repair their own churches and school buildings, too. The Gospel is spreading and is enlightening the dark hearts. The Betsileo tribe was, in those early days, a community of wild heathen. It was not without fear that those two young men took up work there. But God had called them to spread the Gospel among those heathen and He protected them from all the dangers that they so often faced, and He richly blessed their work.

In Tananarive there were many English missionaries who had been working there for a number of years before the Norwegian missionaries arrived. They had written the Malagasy alphabet, which had not been written before. They had also translated the Bible into the Malagasy language and had had it printed. This Bible was later revised. Rev. Lars Dahle, one of the missionaries from Norway, was one of those who accomplished that work, which was finished in 1880. I remember that so well, for I was between 10 and 11 years old at the time.

Now I shall tell more about our own experiences....

Queen Ranavalona II had become a Christian. She did not want the two young Norwegian missionaries to move so far away from the capital city; "for," said she, "the Betsileo tribe is wild and they might kill you." But the two men placed the matter in God's hand and set out, contrary to the wish of the queen.

Looking back over the events of those days, one cannot but realize that it was God who led them. When the queen received the letter telling about their departure into the interior, she sent a message to her subjects, ordering them to give a most hearty welcome to those strangers who had come to live with them and to teach them and their children, because they were her friends. That letter from the queen proved to be of much help and protection. The natives of that region had never before seen white people—*Vazaha*, as they called them. They were, of course, very curious, and all came to see the queer, white-skinned, light-haired, blue-eyed foreigners. "The eyes of the *ngara maso* [the blue-eyed folks] are like cat-eyes," some said. "And what queer feet the foreigners have," they thought, for they imagined that the shoes they wore were a part of their feet. One of the missionaries was even requested to give them a close look at his feet.

The missionaries managed to rent a small one-room house, with an equally small attic which could be entered by means of a rickety ladder that was far from easy to climb. My parents lived up in that attic for some time. Mother said that when food was being cooked in the lower room, it was impossible to be up in the attic. In those days the Malagasy folks had the fireplace in the center of the room in which they lived, so that the members of the family might sit around it and see the kettle boil. The kettle was placed on three fairly high stones, and grass was used for fuel. There was no chimney and the house was so full of smoke that tears kept trickling down one's cheeks. Such was pioneer life among the heathen, but the missionaries did not lose courage.

There was one door to the house, and a small opening for a window. Mother said that when first they came there, so many people crowded at the doors and windows to watch them that it was dark inside; but when they began to eat, the crowds left for awhile, because it is not customary to stand and glare at people while they are eating.

When the curiosity had died down to some extent, it became possible to talk to this one and that one; and when they realized that the foreigners were not dangerous, some became bold enough to come into the house where the missionaries could converse with them and even begin to teach them the alphabet.

Tables and chairs were not to be had. Mr. Engh had brought with him a box of carpenter's tools, but that was stolen on the journey; and the two men who carried it were killed by the robbers. It took some time to get the needed tools, which had to be sent from the capital city.

After some time, they succeeded in building a house where they could meet for services and where the inquirers could come for instruction. There were no schools in those days, and the missionaries had to begin school work. By winning the children for Christ, they could often win the parents, too. The queen issued orders to the effect that parents must send their children to mission schools. That was the first opportunity those Malagasy children had to attend school.

After some time my parents moved to another place—Masinandraina—to open a mission station. That was where a sister of mine, and I, were born. My oldest brother was born in Betafo.

Malagasy workers build a traditional house.

Mother told us that there was no cloth to be had and that she had to take sheets and pillow-cases to make clothes for the little ones.

After some years, new missionaries arrived on the field. Father left them in charge of the station where we had been, and we moved to another place to begin work at Loharano. The church—a long, plain structure—was built on the new location before the family moved there. Well I remember when we first arrived at that place. We camped in a little room with a mud floor—the sacristy of the church—and that was our home for nearly a year, while the residence was under construction. The missionary home was to be built of sun-dried bricks. The bricks had to be made first and left to dry for a long time. I remember when we children once filled a brick mold. How happy we were when the mold was removed and we saw a neatly formed brick lying there.

There was no lumber to be had in the interior, so several men were sent down to the forest near the coast to saw lumber, which was carried by men on their shoulders for several days before they arrived at the new station. The boards were used in the making of doors and window-frames. The window glass, too, had to be carried up from the coast. Slough-grass was used for covering the roof. There were four rooms on the main floor and four up-stairs. In the interior of Madagascar houses are usually made of sun-dried brick or of mud. Wages for workers in those days were very small.

Mail from Norway usually arrived once a year, when the mission ship, *Elieser*, came on its regular journey. The mail was then carried by men 16 days from the coast to the interior. It was even possible to get wheat flour from Norway. That came in sealed tin boxes, each holding about 50 pounds. No wheat flour could be bought where we lived in those days. Mother sometimes managed to get rice pounded quite fine and she mixed that with wheat flour, so we got some bread to eat once in awhile. It was not easy for Father and Mother to get along without bread for their every-day fare; but we children did not miss bread when we could have rice, honey, and milk for breakfast; rice with chicken, meat, or fish for dinner; and rice, again, or pancakes made of rice flour, potatoes, and other vegetables for supper. The rice we got in Madagascar had a better flavor than what we get here [South Dakota]. It is of a pinkish

The Nilsen family in 1887. Top row: Caroline, Antonette, Gabriel, Ommund, and Thomine. Middle row: Inger, Ida, Herman, and Nils. Bottom row: Inga (Inge) and Gertrude. Missing: Ida's twin sister Anna, who died at sea earlier in the year.

The Nilsens dug wells like this one in Loharano, an area rich with natural water springs.

color and has more nutritious value.

Milk could not be bought from the natives. They did not milk their cows, for the calves had to have the milk. Since the cows were not good milk cows, Father had to buy several of them to supply the milk we needed. The cows first refused to give milk, and, in order to get them to do so, Father butchered a calf, stuffed the skin, and placed it in front of the cow when it was to be milked. If the stuffed calf was not there, the cow kept back the milk. A boy was hired to herd the cows.

Even though the weather was warm throughout the year, it was necessary to build a good stable for the cows at night. That was because of thieves. Our cows were often stolen, and had to be replaced. One night the thieves dug a hole in the stable wall, and managed to get the cows out through it. We had two dogs, but the thieves were able to keep them quiet by feeding them meat. Years after that case of robbery we learned that a man whom Father had hired to help us, one who seemed to be so honest and whom we never suspected of stealing, had actually helped his brothers get away with the cows. That was the way he had rewarded Father for all that he had done for him.

The above mentioned man was a slave. He and his wife came and begged for permission to work for us. Again and again he begged Father to help him so that he might become a free man. Father bought him from his master, and then he and his wife worked for us and thus paid back what Father had paid for him. Mother was well pleased because of the deal, for thus she would have much needed help, and would not be changing servants every now and then. Servants were usually so unsteady. When they had worked for a month, or so, and had earned a little money for clothing, they would leave. These two seemed to enjoy working for us, and we enjoyed having them with us, too. They soon showed a desire to learn to read, and every evening after the family devotion Father spent some time instructing them. After the man had learned to read, and had spent some time preparing for baptism, he requested that he might be baptized, and the request was granted. He chose the name Mosesy—Malagasy for "Moses."

Mosesy had some brothers, and they visited with him once in a while. They must have been the ones who led him astray. Strange it seems now that during the time they were with us we lost several of our cows, and the tracks left by the cows led westward, towards the place where their home was, but we never suspected that he or his brothers had stolen the cows. They lived so far away, too.

The cows were usually stolen when Father was away on some of his long journeys to the different outstations and schools. He was often away for a week or more, which gave the man ample time to send word to his brothers. As soon as it was discovered that the cows had disappeared, Mosesy and others were sent to search for them. The cows were not found, but once they did find a young heifer along the way, evidently speared because it had not been able to keep up in the chase.

Finally the time came that Mosesy and his wife were ready to leave us. Their debt was paid, and they were eager to return to their home. The last evening they were with us, Mosesy baked pancakes for our supper. My little sister (one of the twins—about five years old) came to the kitchen door to ask if she might have a pancake, for she was hungry.[5] When she stood in the door and saw that Mosesy and his wife were sitting by the fireplace talking she did not want to disturb them, but stood waiting till they should be through talking. Then she heard Mosesy say to his wife, "This is the last evening that we will be here. Tomorrow we are going home, but the sad part of it is that we are going to an empty house, and we do not own as much as a cow. But," he continued, "do you know what I have thought of doing? Well, after a couple of nights, I shall return and take all the cows from *Vazaha*, and then we will be rich."

Then Sister stepped forward and asked if she might have a pancake. The man seemed startled. "Have you been standing in the doorway?" "Yes," said Sister. "If you now will promise that you will not mention to your papa and mama what you have heard me say, then you shall have a pancake." Sister promised, for she thought that they were only joking.

Later, alas, the man did exactly what he had said he would do.

---

5. Strangely, Antonette does not identify her younger sister here by name, but it must have been either Anna Nilsen (1877-86) or Ida Nilsen (1877-1958). Only one of the twins would survive their missionary experiences in Madagascar.

The third night after they had left, he, and most likely his brothers, came and took all our cows.

Now our milk supply was gone and it was impossible to buy milk from the natives. "Who could have been so rude as to rob the children of the milk supply?" Mother said. Then Sister spoke up: "Mama, now I know who it is that has stolen our cows." "You surely can't know that," said Mother. Sister told her what she had heard Mosesy tell his wife that evening, what she had thought a joke.

A messenger was sent to Mosesy, requesting him to come back, and he was happy to do so, for he thought that they were going to hire him again.

When he came, Father spoke right out: "You have stolen our cows." Mosesy denied most vehemently. "You must know that I could not possibly be so cruel as to rob those beloved children of their milk supply," he said.

Then Mother spoke up. "We have witnesses," she said. "Witnesses! Bring them out then," he said. Mother summoned my little sister and she again told what she had heard him say to his wife that evening.

The man was completely taken off his guard. "I cannot deny any longer," he said humbly, "when a little child can bear witness." He promised to bring the cows back, and he did. He seemed to be very sorry for what he had done, too.

After we returned to Norway, my youngest brother began to attend school.[6] One day the teacher said to the members of his class: "Do any of you remember the story of Moses that we read some time ago? Who will stand up and tell it?" None of them answered. My little brother knew that he could tell something about Mosesy, and so he got up. The teacher was surprised, for my brother had not been there at the time they read the story of Moses from the Bible, but he said, "Go on and tell it." Then my brother said: "Mosesy stole

6. Antonette's youngest brother was Herman Adolf Nilsen (1881-1958). The family returned to Norway for a two-year stay in 1887.

all our cows." The other children burst out laughing, and the teacher had to order them to be quiet.

The little boy from Madagascar was deeply humiliated. He had heard about the doings of Mosesy, and had jumped to the conclusion that that was the "Moses" to whom the teacher referred. Poor boy!

When Father was away on one of his many journeys, Mother had difficulty in sleeping at night, and often lay wondering about the milk cows. There were many of us children and we needed the milk. I remember one night that Mother woke me and said, "Come with me to the south room. I'll have to scare the thieves."

She loaded a gun and fired a shot through the window, and there were actually thieves there! She heard them running and the dogs running after them. The thieves were scared off that night and did not get away with the cows, but they had dug a hole in the wall of the stable.

I thought Mother was very courageous when she could load and handle a gun. She loaded the gun with a crystal salt, so that, if she should chance to strike a thief, he would smart for his iniquity. I stood there cold and shivering with fear that night. Mother was strong and brave and well able to stand the many dangers and trials that pioneer missionaries have to face.

The natives of the district lived in small colonies and villages along rivers and rice fields. Our mission station was on a plain near the center of that settlement. Thus it was not so far for the people to come to church and for their children to come to school. School houses were, of course, built as soon as mission stations were opened. Father taught and supervised the schools. The missionaries were requested to vaccinate all the school children for smallpox. The children came to school quite early and went home at noon. The older children, who had learned to read and write, helped to instruct the beginners. As the years went by, the schools grew and developed. I remember that my oldest brother taught one class for quite some time when he was home on vacation.[7] The missionaries had a private school for their children at Betafo (where the Enghs were working) where we older children attended school. Later,

7. This would have been Gabriel Nicolai Nilsen Isolany (1868-1935), who also became a missionary in Madagascar. He traveled to Stavanger, Norway, for school in 1885.

there was a school opened for us in the capital city.

When the natives had learned to trust the missionaries, they began to come to church quite regularly. And after some time they learned to clean up and wash their clothes. The heathen do not, as a rule, make a practice of that.

Missionaries usually walked, but when traveling long distances they were occasionally carried by palanquin, such as Peter Halvorson in this photo c. 1900.

Once when Father was on one of his journeys, riding in a palanquin carried by four men, closely followed by another man, who was carrying his bedding, food supplies, and a kettle for cooking—necessities that we had to take with us when traveling in those parts, for there were no hotels—they met a group of suspicious-looking natives. The leader, most likely a robber chief, ordered his followers to stop, and stood staring at Father and his carriers scrutinizingly. Evidently they were ready to take possession of the foreigner's belongings. The four men carrying the palanquin stood still for some time, looking at one another, much frightened. But no attack was launched. Finally the robber chief said to his men, "Let us go on." And on they went.

Malagasy warriors travel in small groups, and are usually barefoot. Their characteristic weapon c. 1900 was the club or spear.

During the early years of this mission, a newly arrived missionary began to build a church with mud walls. To build those walls they took well-churned mud and put it on the level ground without a foundation. The first layer was well squared up, about two feet wide and almost two feet high. They would let this mud stand for a few days to dry; then other layers were added, following that method until the walls were completed. Thus it was that it took so long before the walls of the church could be finished. They had dry weather while that work was going on, and that was, of course, what the builders especially desired. The heathen in the community often came to see the work that was going on, and kept asking how long it would take them to finish the building. They were worrying about their rice fields for they were becoming too dry. They felt sure that the white man was keeping the rain back because of that building. One day they said to the missionary: "If you do not let it rain soon, there is going to be a famine here. We will give you only a few days more to consider the matter."

The missionary did his best to explain to them that it is God, our heavenly Father, who rules the rain, but they would not believe that.[8] One morning, three days later, the angry mob came, armed with spears, ordering the missionary to come out. He did come out and spoke to them. Then he led them to the half-finished church, and had a long conversation with them there. He said, "God rules over all. Now we shall pray that He will send rain." God heard his prayer. Clouds began to gather, and before many of those men got back to their homes, heavy rain began to fall. The men started to laugh and some of them said: "See! He did allow it to rain when we threatened to kill him and his wife and child."

Here I want to tell you something that a German lady once told me about God's protecting hand. Her grandfather was a missionary somewhere in Africa. He came to a tribe of wild heathen to proclaim the Gospel message. The natives did not want him there, and often tried to talk him into leaving their community, but the missionary refused to leave. Finally, one evening, the members of

---

8. One of the primary functions of the priest class in Malagasy traditional religion is rain making, which Peter Halvorson described as being facilitated by the priest's *ody*—that is, magic means or medicine.

the tribe went to the place where he lived, intending to kill him. As they were nearing the place, they were all surprised and frightened, for they saw a circle of white-robed angels, armed with shining swords, surrounding the house. They were terror stricken and fled. Many years later some of those men were won for Christ, and then they told the missionary what had taken place on the evening they had planned to kill him, and about what they had seen. God saves His witnesses in many wonderful ways.

In those days the towns of the Malagasy people were fortified by cactus hedges above five or six feet wide. The towns were not large; there were twenty or thirty huts in each. Outside of the hedges deep ditches were dug to prevent robbers from getting in. There was one large, strong gate, and that was closed in the evenings and a huge stone was rolled in front of it.

The people who lived in town who owned cattle usually gathered them into a hollowed-out place. When it rained the cattle stood in deep mud all night long. Those who owned a pig or two, and some sheep, chickens, etc., kept them in the house where they lived. They usually build a separate room for the pigs in a corner of their entrance, and on the top of that, a room for the sheep and chickens, to prevent thieves from stealing them.

Many times we have spent nights in that kind of home, when traveling to, or from, our school at Tananarive, which took us three days and two nights. The nights

Much of the plant life encountered in Madagascar is unique to the island, such as this spiny foliage, which can be used for protection.

31

were spent in homes like those mentioned above, where the cocks were crowing most of the night, and where the air was very foul.[9]

Robbers were very numerous in those days. A Malagasy never felt safe, and was constantly worrying about robber attacks. All the men carried spears and knives. And quite frequently robber bands launched attacks on towns at night, looted the homes, and set them on fire. Those of the citizens who were unable to flee were taken captive, especially women and children. The cattle were, of course, stolen. The men, often unable to protect their families, usually managed to make their escape. When the robbers returned to their home communities, they divided the booty with their neighbors, and many mothers and children were thus separated and kept as slaves.

Well do I remember how town after town in the district where we were living—Loharano—was raided. These robber raids were carried on over the entire island until France took over Madagascar as a colony in 1895, and soon put an end to that lawless practice.

No matter how well fortified with cactus hedges the towns were, the robbers chopped their way through the hedges, crossed over the cactus and ditches on boards that they carried with them, and broke open the gates. Our home was the only unfortified home in the district; anybody could enter there, but God protected His witnesses in such marvelous ways.

One night Mother awoke to discover that fire had broken out at our station. When she came outside, she saw three enclosures on the mission compound—the school house, a wood shed, and our stable—were burning. Two men were at the door, and they insisted on going up-stairs that they might keep the fire from spreading to the roof. Mother could not trust those men, and said, "No!" She could see that the wind did not come from the direction of the burning houses. Later, when we found out who had started the fires, we learned that those two men had planned to burn down the house we lived in, too.

Father hurried to the stable, between the other two burning

---

9. The habit of living with animals was common in 19th-century Norway too, but there the animals usually lived in enclosures below the house proper. In Africa, living indoors with animals that are penned in a corner is still common in the smaller villages, and this arrangement is a leading cause of tuberculosis.

houses, to open the door and rescue the cattle. The herd-boy threw the key to him, but he threw it too far so that it landed on the roof. Father kicked the door open so that the cows got out. Some of the calves were burned to death, however; for there was one door that Father could not get open. Soon many people from the small towns nearby gathered around us. How could they have seen the fire, or even heard about it? And we were so far away that they could not have heard the shouting. But there they were. They took the calves that had been burned to death, cut them asunder with their long knives and their spears (weapons that the natives always carried with them). They spent the rest of the night in roasting the veal and feasting upon it.

While the people were busy roasting and feasting, the two above mentioned men (a father and son) went behind our house, broke open a small window leading to a closet, stole our clothes and a large chunk of soap (made by Malagasy people). Some time later we began to suspect that it was those two men who had done it. They went about peddling small pieces of soap, and soap making was not their trade. People became suspicious and told us about the matter. The men were summoned and questioned, and they finally confessed that they had been stealing. They were the men whom Father took with him when he set out on long journeys to visit schools and churches. They were always ready to go, and they got other men to help, too. When Father got home again, he usually went into the closet and brought out money to pay them. Once they were reported to have said that they no longer needed to work for *Vazaha* (the white man), for now they knew where he kept his money. Evidently it was money that they were in hopes of getting that night, but they did not find the key, though it was hanging on a nail close at hand.

These men felt sorry for what they had done, and after some time they came and begged for help to learn to read and to prepare for baptism.

We took into our living quarters those who had lost their rooms when those houses were burned down. They were an assistant teacher, one who taught singing, the shepherd boy, our cook, and his wife. They occupied two rooms downstairs during the night.

As a rule Father did not lock our bedroom door in the evenings when he came up to go to bed, though Mother often suggested that he do so. He sometimes answered, "Oh, well, there is no danger." One evening when he came up, Mother heard him lock the door. It certainly was God who caused him to lock the door that time, and Father did not even recall that he had done so. A peculiar feeling of anxiety crept over Mother. She had a premonition that something was going to happen that night, and she lay awake, unable to sleep.

After some time, Mother heard someone coming up the stairs, and then trying to open the door. Father was surprised that the door was locked. He asked who was at the door, but received no answer. Someone kept working with the lock, evidently expecting to get the door open. Finally the unexpected visitor spoke up, "It is I, the teacher. Open the door for me! I am afraid to be downstairs! There must be robbers outside!"

"No," answered Mother. "If there were robbers outside, we would have heard them. We have two dogs, and I haven't heard them bark once." She went out on the veranda and called to the dogs, and there they were just outside the door. After half an hour or so Mother heard the intruder go downstairs again.

The following morning Father asked the man what he had planned to do, but he would not answer.

"Oh, yes," said Father, "your intention was to kill us and steal our possessions. And you were not alone. Others were with you." Then Father paid him and his companions their wages and sent them away. That time, too, God protected us in a most marvelous manner.

It saddened Mother to send away this couple who had helped to take care of us children. Everything was so unhandy that Mother was much in need of help. When washing clothes, for instance, they had to go down to the nearby river and beat the clothes against a rock. No washboards or tubs were to be had. The clothes had to be rinsed in the river, and for that a man's help was needed. Servants were needed to go on errands, too—to the market place for supplies, etc. Now the problem was to find new servants and to train them, which took time. They must get the proper clothes in which to attire themselves so as to appear somewhat neat, and they must be taught cleanliness, for nothing seemed to be too filthy for the natives. It was far from pleasant to have them around before they learned to keep clean.

When Father sent to the mission secretary, who lived in Antsirabe—a three-hour walk from our station—to get money, he sent a Christian by the name of Daniela. I remember him so well. When setting out on that expedition he would attire himself in a filthy, ragged gunny-sack, and carry an old, shabby basket on a stick across his

Two Malagasy men carry food using hardwood carriers.

shoulder. Again and again he went on that errand for Father and brought back the needed funds. No robbers thought it worth while to hold him up, for they must have taken him for a poverty stricken old man. He never told anybody about his errands, and thus he was able to keep that job for a long time.

Father usually made our tallow candles, with the whole family watching him, and doing their best to help. When evening came and the candles were ready, we had many hundreds of them. We owned only one lamp, for kerosene was very expensive in those days. It was brought from the coast, carried on the shoulders of men all that distance. The men of Madagascar are very sturdy when it comes to carrying heavy burdens day after day from the coast to the interior of the island. The journey from the coast to the capital city took about two weeks. There was no railroad on the island in these days, nor were there wagons to be pulled by horses or oxen. The first missionaries made their way into the interior to where we were by carriers [palanquins].

That long, tiresome journey was especially trying because they had not learned much of the language. Mother said that she managed to find out how to say, "What is this called?" She kept asking her carriers what they called this and what they called that, and then she wrote down the answers they gave. Thus she managed to learn quite a few words and sentences. On that journey she traveled together with Mrs. Engh, Mr. Borgen, and Bishop Schreuder, who came from Africa on board the *Elieser*.[10]

The natives lived mainly on rice, sweet potatoes, *sonzo* (another kind of potato), and *Kasava* (a very tasty root from which tapioca is produced). It is dried before it is cooked and is very tasty, as well as nutritious. When the natives are out traveling they use *Kasava* as bread. It is usually sold to travelers at market places. The natives use many different kinds of vegetables that grow wild. As to fruits, they can get bananas the year round. The banana palm produces only one bunch of fruit, and when that is hewn off, the stem withers and

dies. A new one soon springs up, however, which will grow and develop and bear fruit. Some kinds of lemons grow wild in the woods, especially in the brush-wood along the coast and on the mountain sides. Wild raspber-

The beauty of produce on market days, including rice, bananas, coconuts, corn, and root vegetables.

10. This inland trip took place in 1867, shortly after the missionaries' brides-to-be had arrived. Bishop Hans Schreuder, an early missionary to South Africa, brought the women inland with Nils Nilsen and John Engh, and examined potential mission sites with them.

ries and other berries are quite abundant. Oranges, mangoes, figs, and other kinds of tropical fruit trees also grow here. A great deal of sugarcane is raised to produce sugar and syrup; it also serves as candy, for people make a practice of chewing it and sucking out the sweet juice.

Madagascar is said to have the greatest variety of palm trees, growing mainly along the coast. Coconut palms are plentiful, and thrive best near the coast where the air is salty.

The lemur (*maky*) is a kind of monkey that is found only in Madagascar, so they say. They stay in the woods, but they are more tame than other monkeys, so that children can often play with them.[11]

Lemurs near Ft. Dauphin today.

Birds of giant size used to live there. They grew to a height of from 10 to 14 feet, and were far taller than any ostrich. A bird of that kind is called an *Aepyornis*. It is believed that the last of the birds died more than 200 years ago. Yet their eggs are located by natives who search for them. Such an egg may measure up to 14 inches long. The shell is large enough to hold 6 times as much as an ostrich egg, or as much as 12 dozen hen's

Two elephant bird eggs (*Aepyornis maximus*) are compared with an ostrich egg and two crocodile eggs.

eggs. The one we had with us can be seen at the Museum of South Dakota University.

Crocodiles and wild pigs are the only dangerous animals. There are no poisonous snakes.

Cotton and hemp are raised in Madagascar. In former days many of the people wove their own *lamba* from these products.

11. For example, Antonette's daughter Ruth Halvorson Berge (1907-96) had a beloved pet lemur named Koto, who often rode on Ruth's shoulders as she explored the tropical surroundings.

P. C. Halvorson stands by a crocodile he shot, c. 1900.

A sort of wild silk was found in a certain forest, and was used in making silk *lambas*. The Chinese silkworm must be cared for in the house and fed on mulberry leaves. It takes a month from the time the eggs are hatched until the cocoons are spun. It certainly was interesting to see how the silkworms grew and developed.

The native women used slough-grass for weaving rugs and baskets. Mother sent for a loom and a spinning wheel and was fortunate enough to get them. They arrived on the ship *Elieser*. She wove cotton blankets for us and knit our stockings.

We did not have a stove so all the cooking was done on the open fireplace, in a large iron kettle. When we were able to get flour, bread and cakes were also baked in it. I remember so well the time Mother baked a cake when the twins were to be baptized. The twins, Anna and Ida, were seven years younger than I.

It did not happen very often that we saw other white children. Father went to the different places each year to attend the annual pastors' conference, and once in awhile the family went with him, when it was not too far to travel. We children enjoyed those journeys immensely, and on those occasions we had the joy of seeing other white children.

At times we went to the hot-water bath at Antisirabe, about a three-hour walk from where we lived, and stayed there for some weeks. Those baths were especially good for Mother. Once when we

Malagasy hunters display a wild boar (wild pig).

were there, a prince—Ramahitra—was also there.[12] He had, of course, come from the capital city. As we children were playing, we chanced to go into Ramahitra's yard. He stood in the door, watching us. Suddenly he called to us and asked us to come over to where he was. He gave us some candy out of a large glass jar. He told us to hold out both hands and then he poured them full of the most delicious candy. That was the first candy that I had ever tasted, and I was between seven and eight years at the time. There was no candy to be had where we were those days. The Malagasy children often used to suck at little lumps of salt, whenever they could get them, which was not very often, for that, too, came from the coast, and was very expensive.

ACTIVITY AMONG THE LEPERS

A home for people suffering from leprosy was established at Antsirabe; there were many lepers in this territory. Missionary Rosaas arranged for the building of several homes to receive these unfortunate and helpless human beings living in filthy caves of extreme misery until death brought relief. With the building of a

12. Peter Halvorson describes a prince named Ramahatra who was the Malagasy minister of war shortly before France annexed Madagascar as a colony (see Chapter 6). Halvorson describes the prince as a significant leader who came to southern Madagascar to investigate governmental corruption. Is this the same man that Antonette met several years earlier?

Tananarive, the capital, in earlier times.

hospital and a church, as well as the arrival of several Deaconesses from Norway, a great act of mercy was performed among these leprous people. Among the Deaconesses rendering this Christian service was Maria Foreid; she was the first nurse in this territory and served faithfully for thirty years. After the first station was destroyed by fire during an uprising, another location was chosen where the surroundings were more favorable. This is a beautiful place, with sufficient room and facilities for hundreds of leprous men and women.

QUEEN RANAVALONA III

The queen and the prime minister each had a castle on the highest point in the capital city, where they could be seen from far off. An English architect had supervised the building of those beautiful castles.[13] A huge clock which was sent to the queen from a European country was put up in the steeple of the queen's castle. The mission secretary, Rev. Lars Dahle, had the honor of presenting the gift to the queen. I saw the clock. We were there when Rev. Dahle opened the box in which it came, to see that everything was in good condition before it was delivered. That was when Queen Ranavalona II was still living.

Just below the castle there is a level plain—*Mahamasina*—and in the center of that was a high, rounded rock where kings and queens had been crowned for generations back. The last queen of Madagascar—Ranavalona III—was crowned in the year 1883. I was there that day.

There was a platform built beside the rock, and there the high officials and English and Norwegian missionaries were seated. I sat

13. The architect who originally constructed the Queen's Palace in Tananarive was the Frenchman Jean Laborde, who used a 130-foot-tall tree trunk in the mostly wooden structure. Antonette seems to be describing here one of the castle additions. Unfortunately, the palace burned to the ground in 1995. See Tyson, *The Eighth Continent*, p. 10.

so near the queen that I could plainly hear her speech and that of the prime minister.[14]

The queen had been educated at a Quaker Mission School. A group of girls from the Norwegian Mission School—Mrs. Borchgrevink's pupils—were there and sang a song on the program.

The prime minister was attired in a white silk suit. He was the main speaker. This took place at the time that France was trying to get possession of the island, so the prime minister said in his

Queen Ranavalona III, coronated in 1883, from a photograph in Antonette's collection.

message: "Fear not, Ranavalona. We will protect your kingdom. The French shall not get so much as a hand's breadth of this land." Then he turned to the audience and called out, "Isn't that so, good people." And the people shouted with one accord, "Yes, that is so!"

Then the queen arose and delivered her message. Among other things she said: "I thank you all for your willingness to defend our country, and for your loyalty."

When the program was over the queen was to ride in a little buggy drawn by a beautiful white horse, so that the people might have a chance to see her. I don't think that horse had ever pulled a buggy before. In spite of the fact that many officers were holding the horse and the buggy, he made a sudden leap, and off fell the queen's crown. I can still see that scene, for we children had run over to be as near as we could get when she climbed into the buggy.

"Bad luck!" said one man. "She will lose her crown," said another. The people seemed sad and disappointed. The horse was unhitched, and the officers pulled the buggy so that the many

14. In other words, there were no microphones or speakers to amplify the voices. The prime minister at this time was a man named Rainilaiarivony. He held much of the power in Madagascar, and married (successively) Radama II's widow Rasoherina, Ranavalona II, and Ranavalona III.

thousands of people gathered on the plain could see the queen.

Ranavalona III was 22 years old at the time of her coronation. People said that she was not happy. We saw her on several occasions, and she did look sad. She had been happily married before her coronation, and now she was to be married to the prime minister. Her first husband had disappeared after the death of the former queen. It was said that he had been mysteriously murdered. Now she was to be queen because she was of the royal family.

Ranavalona III lost her kingdom, as people that day feared that she would. She ruled for 12 years. In 1895 the French took possession of the island, and she was banished to Algiers in North Africa where she died a few years later, most likely because of sorrow.[15] None of her relatives were permitted to be with her. Some of her relatives were among my best friends there.

Schools for Missionaries' Children

After some time schools for missionaries' children were opened in the capital city, and we had to make the three-day journey to attend school the greater part of the year, being at home only during the three-months' vacation.

Our teachers were: Missionary Joseph Nilsen, beloved by us all; Miss Franzen, an especially gifted and noble woman; and the excellent housekeeper, Miss Anna Tingwold, who had charge of the cooking department. She was assisted by native servants. There were 12 of us children the first year. Others arrived later.

The school building was rented. It was a large three-story house not often seen in those days. The school rooms were on the main floor. The school compound was quite large. A high mud wall surrounded each house or group of houses, as the custom was there. In the garden coffee bushes grew which supplied enough for our teachers. We children were given a cup of coffee each Sunday as a special favor.

We had a rich supply of flowers. Each of us girls had a little flowerbed of our own. On Saturday we took care of them and pre-

15. Ranavalona III was exiled to the French island of Reunion in 1897 and transferred to Algeria in 1899, where she died.

pared bouquets that we brought with us to church on Sunday morning, mainly to decorate the graves.

The church was built on a high hill—*Ambatovinaky* ("chiseled rock"). It was not easy to climb up that steep road in the heat, but then going down the hill was easy. There was a Norwegian congregation in the capital city, and a printing office, a hospital, and a school for boys, of which a Mr. Borgen had charge.[16] Also a girls' school with Mrs. Borchgrevink in charge. (These schools are not there now.)

Dr. Borchgrevink was a medical missionary, and was highly esteemed by the Malagasy people, and others as well. Mr. L. Dahle was the one who began the theological seminary for native boys there. Those two were the first Norwegian missionaries in the capital city. I remember when the *Ambatovinaky* church was dedicated. Missionary Engh was its master builder. My parents came to be present at the dedication. I was between five and six years old at the time.[17]

When we children went home for vacation, our teacher escorted us, and then our parents came to meet us at a place agreed upon. When crossing rivers where there were no bridges, we were placed on the shoulders of carriers, and they waded through the deep waters. Their feet were steady and they got through safely with their heavy burdens. We children looked forward to these journeys with much joy. It was like a picnic to be carried in a palanquin or chair with long bamboo poles attached to both sides, with four men carrying it on their shoulders. It was a slow but fairly safe mode of travel. The carriers were strong and sturdy and fleet of foot.

Once in a while our teacher took us for boat rides on the river, through the green woodlands, a few miles outside of the city. Once he took us older children with him to the church where the queen attended services. A Malagasy pastor was in charge of that congregation. As we entered the church, we had a chance to shake hands with the queen, and that was a great honor. When we returned, we told the servants about that wonderful event.

16. This may be the same Mr. Borgen that originally accompanied Antonette's mother Inger and Mrs. Engh, along with Bishop Schreuder, when the brides-to-be first arrived in Madagascar in 1867.
17. That is, the dedication would have been in 1875 or 1876.

"Did you press her hand as hard as you usually do?" asked one of the servants.

"Yes, I guess we did," was our answer.

One evening the queen invited many people and all the missionaries to the city to a festive gathering in the palace to celebrate a national festivity. The main floor of the castle was one large room with many pillars. All the guests sat on the floor. Only the queen and her attendants had chairs. A nationally festive meal was served—a plateful of rice and honey, and dried meat that was a year old.

SPECIAL FESTIVITIES

Pioneer missionaries, in order to gain the confidence of the natives when beginning work in a new place, would invite them for a meal at Christmas time. Usually the natives were afraid of the foreigners—the *Vazaha*—as they called them. Those festive occasions served as bonds of confidence between them. At first, the natives were reluctant about accepting the invitation, but by the next Christmas season more were added to the group. When the meal was over, the missionaries conducted devotional services, and encouraged their guests to attend church services, listen to the Word of God, and send their children to school. I remember some of those festivities. That custom was discontinued later on, however.

There were many on the committee to arrange for those festivities. An ox was butchered, and there would be rice. An ox could be had for only a few dollars. I remember so well the many pots and pans here and there out in the yard where meat and rice were cooking. The rice had to be scorched a bit to suit the natives. Then it has an especially good taste and smell.

According to Malagasy customs (I am writing mainly about bygone days), the skin of the ox was cooked with the meat, for that, too, was "meat," and so were the intestines. They were washed in the river and cut in pieces. That was supposed to add special flavor to the meat, according to Malagasy taste. For us a special kettle of meat was prepared, and we, too, ate with our guests.

Several long mats were spread on the ground, and they served as plates. Rice was "dished out" on the mats, and the meat

Carts pulled by oxen continue to be a major form of transportation in Madagascar.

and gravy on top of it. The people sat on both sides of the mats. They took the meat with their fingers when they ate. One difficult problem was to get spoons for so many guests. Some had probably brought spoons with them. When spoons were lacking, a group would eat with one spoon, passing it from one to another. Each would take a large spoonful, and then pass the spoon on to the next man. Then they kept chewing meat till the spoon came around again. A dipper filled with water also went from mouth to mouth, but when the Malagasy folks are served meat, it is a real feat. One of their customs is not to talk when they eat. They smack their lips in appreciation. We children usually stood around and took it all in. I remember how the committee divided the rice to those seated at the different mats. Now and then someone made a rice ball, rolling the hot rice between his hands till it looked like an ice cream cone. Those they presented to me and to the other children, usually saying, "Probably you, too, are hungry." I know that I ate them with relish then, but I should not be able to swallow them now.

As the years went by, the people came to the mission station at Loharano in great numbers to learn to read, study the Word of God,

45

and prepare for baptism.[18] Father had the joy of seeing much fruit of his work. God blessed it richly. Large congregations were organized in the district. Well I remember what joy it was to see the people pouring into the church on Sunday mornings—neatly dressed people from north and south, east and west. The church was usually well filled. A hymn that Father had composed[19] was often sung:

Miambena, re,   Miambena, re,
Ry fanahiko.   Ry fanahiko,
Misy rafinao Misaina   Mba tsy ho andevon'ota,
Hanangoly ny Malaina   Na ho taomin'ny mpanota;
Be ny fandrika   Mivavaha, re,
Voavelatra.   Ry fanahiko!

The man who felt that it was his duty to keep the people orderly in church did not find it necessary to continue that work very long. People soon learned to keep quiet when in church.

My sister, Caroline, and I were confirmed in that congregation.[20] I remember how still and devotional the people were. We were confirmed in the Norwegian language, and the natives did not understand what was said, but they sat there very quiet and orderly.

My brother, Gabriel, was confirmed the previous year, and that same year went to Norway with some of the missionaries.

In the churchyard there is a lonely little grave. Herman, a little brother of mine, passed away when he was only a week old.[21]

Father had planted many trees in the mission compound at Loharano and among them were several eucalyptus trees. He had brought the seed with him from Africa. Now those beautiful trees are spreading over the island—a memorial to my father.

---

18. Since the Protestant Reformation of the 16th century, Lutheran evangelism has been closely related to basic instruction in reading and studying the Bible.
19. Three hymns in the present hymnal of the Malagasy Lutheran Church were written by Nils Nilsen.
20. Caroline Nilsen (1871-1952), who was one year younger than Antonette, would also return to Madagascar as a missionary in adulthood. (She worked at the Ft. Dauphin mission from 1894 to 1901.) The two girls were apparently confirmed together in 1886.
21. A second Herman was later born and survived—Herman Adolf Nilsen.

A group of Malagasy men and Lutheran missionaries stand by an old baobab tree.

The work at the Loharano mission station was greatly blessed by God. In 1946, when the congregation celebrated its 75th anniversary, 5,000 Malagasy Christians gathered from the North Betsileo district for this event. The natives were in full charge of the meetings, the missionaries staying in the background and speaking only when requested to do so by the committee in charge. A chorus of 490 voices sang an arrangement of the 150th Psalm. All the surrounding villages had offered to accommodate guests and the things needed during their four days' stay, including firewood. They also had gathered 18 tons of rice and butchered 8 oxen.

CHAPTER 2
OFF TO OTHER FIELDS OF WORK

FINALLY THE TIME CAME WHEN WE WERE TO LEAVE LOHARANO ("THE WATER SPRING"). Father and Mother had worked about 20 years on that mission field. Missionary Engh and his wife came out with them, and now they, with their families, went home together. The Malagasy people, especially the Christians, were much saddened to see them leave.

For many years Father received letters from Randriamanga, the first Malagasy that he had baptized, who was a young boy at that time. Later he became an especially good helper, and an assistant teacher. Both he and his good wife, Ramaria, were of great help in the work. They were very much interested in the church and the congregation. They were the first visible fruit of Father's work. Randriamanga became blind in his old age, and was taken to a home for blind people that had been opened at Loharano.

On October 5, 1886, we journeyed down to the coast, to Mananzary, a poor harbor on the east coast of the island, where the mission ship that was to take us home was to anchor, a new sailing vessel, the *Paulus* (somewhat larger than the *Elieser*, and on its first voyage). After a week of difficult travel, we stopped for two weeks to visit with fellow missionaries at Fianarantsoa, in South Betsileo, where the Norwegian mission has its theological seminary. Our station was in North Betsileo.

The good sailboat *Paulus*, which carried the Nilsens and other missionaries between Norway and Madagascar.

We formed quite a large caravan on that journey. Many men carried our luggage—our clothing, blankets, kettles, etc. At night we camped in shabby little huts. We secured clean mats, spread out blankets on them, and slept on the floor. We children slept fairly well, but it was not so easy for Father and Mother to sleep on hard clay floors. It took three weeks to make that journey in palanquins. Father got a Christian man to look after our baggage (otherwise the carriers might have disappeared into the forest with their burdens). We got through safely with all our luggage. The man who was in charge of our baggage asked for permission to go with us on board the ship so that he would see how we were to fare there. He was seasick during the night that he spent on board, and was happy to go on shore again the following day. He said to Father: "Now I know that if you missionaries did not have the love of Christ, you would not have wanted to come to us on board a ship, and suffer so for many weeks. I had enough of it last night."

It was three days before all who were to travel with us had come on board ship (which was anchored several miles out at sea, for there was no harbor).

The missionaries who sailed on that voyage were the Enghs, and their eight children; the Minsaas, and their three children; Mrs. Haslund, a widow, and her three children; Miss Anna Tingwold; and Father and Mother and their nine children. We watched closely as the first boat took passengers out to the ship. At times we lost sight of it, and feared that it had been swallowed up by the waves. The following morning it was our turn to get into the boat. They could make only one trip out to the ship each day. We set out early in the

Long boats bring in supplies from larger ships in the harbor.

morning, because later in the day the waves became so high that it was impossible to row. It was a most dangerous journey for the boat, which was rowed by several men from the river and out to the open sea. We sat holding each other's hands, for there was not much of a railing along the sides of the boat, and we clung to a rope so as not to roll off.

After boarding the *Paulus* we soon began to be seasick, and, before long, were lying in a corner on the deck. Then the first mate came and took my sister and me for a walk along the deck. We walked until we began to feel very tired. That is supposed to be a remedy for seasickness. After that walk we did begin to feel better.

When the sails of the *Paulus* were hoisted, and the anchor was lifted, we went in a southeasterly direction, towards the island Mauritius. From the British coast, ships had brought salt that was to be exchanged for brown sugar. It took the ship three weeks to make that trip, for we had to face a strong gale.

Three persons died on that trip. The first was a sister of mine, Anna (one of the twins). She was nine years old. She died of malaria that she and some of the other children had contracted on the journey toward the coast. Our parents and three of us children did not contract the fever. Mother was very seasick. Father was seasick, too, but he was able to be up and around to help care for those who were more sick than he was.

We had been on the ship a week when my sister died. The following day Mrs. Minsaas died. She was suffering from cancer of the throat, and they were going home to seek medical treatment. Her sickness grew worse after their journey to the coast, and there was no doctor on board the ship.

Coffins were made for those two, and they were lowered into the sea. Oh, it was sad to see them sink and then to sail on without them!

After the funeral, Missionary Minsaas had a very serious attack of fever and was bedridden for two weeks. He died the day we first came within sight of the island Mauritius. We thought that he would be buried on shore, but soon found out that he could not be. The ship was quarantined as soon as it reached the harbor, because there were so many sick people and casualties on board. Orders were given to bury him at least seven miles out at sea. The body was wrapped in sailcloth, and several of the fellow passengers went in the ship's boat that took him away. My Father delivered the funeral sermon on board the ship.

There were three Minsaas boys, one nine years old, one six, and one four. It certainly was hard for them to lose their parents. Poor little boys! Miss Anna Tingwold took charge of the boys. She was on her way home to be married, and so the boys got a good home. One of them, Ole (the second of the three), eventually became a missionary and worked at the station where his parents had worked. He died there after four years of service.

The ship *Paulus* remained at the island for six weeks. It was placed in dry dock shortly after the quarantine, and was scraped and painted. In the meantime the salt was unloaded and brown sugar was loaded on. The sailors were busy all day long, dumping the sugar down into the freight room and shoving the freight together into the proper places. They tripped along barefooted, chewing tobacco, and spitting here and there as they were working. We children stood on deck, looking down into the freight room, watching the men.

"Are you spitting on the sugar, too?" we shouted. "You mustn't do that!"

"Yes," was their answer. "We can't run up on deck to spit! We have to work!" For many years after that I did not eat brown sugar or coarse salt.

We remained on board the *Paulus* even when the ship was in dry dock. There was a bridge from the ship to land, and we made many visits to the beautiful park not far away, where there were large flower gardens and coconut trees. There was a market place, too, that was especially beautiful. The tables there were decorated with flowers and all kinds of perfumes. We brought with us to Norway fragrant perfumes from that "Land of Perfumes."

Many of the fever stricken passengers were brought to hospitals. My sister, Gertrude, was one of them. She was only three years old, and could not be left alone among the strangers there, so my sister, Caroline, and I took turns being with her. We had to be dressed in hospital garments, like the sick folks, when we were there.

Those were long and dreary days for us. It was a Catholic hospital with many Sisters. One day they showed me their chapel. They were very kind to us. One Catholic priest who visited the sick sent my sister a toy, which certainly was kind. They spoke French and English there, and at that time I did not understand either of those languages.

One morning a Norwegian policeman came to the hospital and spoke to me in the Norwegian language. I had not expected to hear anyone speak in the Norwegian language and did not notice what he said, but answered in the few English words that I had learned, trying to explain that I couldn't speak English. Then the policeman began to laugh and said, "But I spoke Norwegian." I felt ashamed of myself, of course. He came to the hospital several times while we were there, and often teased me about that.

On February 7, 1887, all the sails of the *Paulus* were hoisted and the wind filled them. The ship certainly looked fine. On the prow of the ship was a statue which was supposed to represent St. Paul. It took three months to travel from Mauritius to Liverpool, England. We did not stop anywhere on that journey. We had enough of all necessities in the line of food. We even had fresh meat now and then, for they had two pigs on board which they butchered. We went through storms, and we were delayed by calms. At times we were within sight of other ships and conversed by means of the flag alphabet. Once our captain went to visit another ship in a boat rowed by two members of the crew. Captains of other vessels came to ours for visits, too. The ship rocked more when it stood still than when driven forward by the wind. One day a fresh breeze sprang up and the sailors began pulling the ropes to hoist the sails. We children always enjoyed watching when they were hoisting the sails. During storms we were not permitted to be on deck.

Once we ran short of drinking water so that it became necessary to pump sea water into a large tank in the kitchen so that it might be boiled and distilled. We children volunteered to help, and it might be that we were only in the way, but we were permitted to watch. Rain water was gathered from the sails into an iron tank and also prepared for drinking.

Captain Ludvikson and the sailors were Christians, so we were like one big family. They were fine folks—every one of them. All but one was Norwegian. The cabin boy was Irish, but he, too, could speak Norwegian. I received photographs of the captain and the whole crew.

We celebrated Christmas when we were on the island of Mauritius. The captain went on shore to find a Christmas tree. When he came back he said, "I bought the prettiest tree I could find"—it was a beautiful tree with red leaves.

We sailed along the western coast of Africa, and much of the time we were within sight of land. We saw St. Helena at a distance.[22] Birds from the land often came flying towards the ship, and fluttered around the sails. Sometimes small flying fish fell on the deck and we were able to examine them closely. Now and then we could see huge whales that followed the ship. Sometimes folks on board fished, so we had fried fish to eat.

Though the journey was long, we all enjoyed the days on board the *Paulus*. It was intensely interesting, and a journey that I shall never forget. Mother was well the whole trip, but to her the journey seemed much too long, for Father could not travel with us from Mauritius because of my sister's illness. She had to be under a

22. St. Helena is an island in the South Atlantic off the coast of Angola in West Africa. It was under British control at this time and is also remembered as the place of Napoleon's exile from 1815 to 1821.

The Nilsen family in Washington State (near Battleground) around the time of Peter and Antonette's wedding (c.1896). From left: Nils Nilsen, Antonette, Peter Halvorson, Inger Nilsen, Ommund, Ida, Thomine (Mina), Inge, Herman, and Gertrude The Nilsen children Gabriel and Caroline (Lina) were en route to Madagascar.

doctor's care and there was no doctor on our sailing vessel. My sister, Caroline, went with them, too. They landed in Cape Town, South Africa, and remained there for more than two months, for they did not want to arrive in Norway during the winter season. On May 5 they arrived at Stavanger, Norway, and we arrived there a few days later. We left the island of Mauritius about the same time, but they went on a steamship and we on a sailing vessel.[23]

When we arrived at Liverpool, the wharf was crowded with people who came mainly to see the *Paulus* sail in. We, who had been accustomed to seeing so many dark people, thought it strange to see so many people of our own race. There, in the harbor, we saw the large ship *Eldorado* that had laid the cable line from America and Africa to England.

We stopped at Liverpool to buy clothes, for we had come attired in the clothes that we wore in the tropical regions, so when we arrived at Stavanger, people sized us up as Britishers.

When we were at Liverpool, we saw the large wax cabinet. At

23. That is, the steamship was much faster than the sailing ship, which was at the mercy of the winds.

Mother Inger Nilsen, along with daughter Gertrude and her sisters, watch the cattle about 3.5 miles east of Battleground, Washington.

the entrance stood a very life-like statue—a policeman with a child in his arms. The child was crying, and the policeman was offering him a red apple. When we were ready to enter the building, Mother said, "Wait a bit, I want to speak to that policeman first." When we told her that it was not a living man, she was very much surprised and said, "Now I have seen enough. I don't want to go in." We tried to talk her into going in with us, and finally she did consent, but Mother did not seem to be very enthusiastic that evening.

We left the *Paulus* and took a train to Hull [on the east coast of England], where we boarded a steamer that brought us to Norway. For two years we lived in Stavanger. One summer we went with father to visit his relatives near Bergen, Arnevaag, and other places. The following summer we visited Mother's relatives in Sogndalen. We certainly enjoyed ourselves in beautiful Norway!

After our two-year sojourn in Norway, the entire family migrated to America, to the state of Washington. That was in 1889. My parents bought a little country home and lived there the rest of their lives. Mother passed away at the age of 75. Father lived until he was nearing his 90th birthday.[24]

24. Inger Omundsdotter Heskestad (1845-1921) and Nils Nilsen Staveness (1834-1923) are buried in a pioneer cemetery in Ridgefield, Washington.

Almost all of my folks lived on the West Coast. Two of my brothers—Gabriel and Ommund—and my sister, Tomine, died there. The others—Caroline, Ida, Gertrude, Inge, and Herman—are living there.[25]

Eight years after coming to America, I married Rev. Peter C. Halvorson of Sinai, South Dakota—in 1896. He was called as a missionary to Ft. Dauphin, Madagascar, where he was to be in charge of a school for boys.

My brother, Gabriel Nilsen Isolany, was also called as a missionary to Ft. Dauphin, Madagascar. Likewise my sister, Caroline Nilsen.

Rev. Isolany was married to my husband's sister, Inga Halvorson, and these three left for the mission field in 1893.[26]

Back row: Caroline Nilsen, J. Skaar, and Mrs. Skaar. Front row: Gabriel and Inga Isolany, Eugene Rateaver, Antonette and P. C. Halvorson.

25. Gabriel Nilsen Isolany (1868-1935), Ommund Nilsen (1873-1939), Thomine Nilsen Heitman (1875-1942), Caroline Nilsen (1871-1952), Ida Nilsen Glarum (1877-1958), Gertrude Nilsen Christensen (1883-1965), Inge Nilsen Heitman (1885-1977), Herman Nilsen (1881-1958).
26. Gabriel Nilsen Isolany and Inga Halvorson Isolany (1872-1937) were missionaries in Madagascar from 1893 to 1901. Gabriel acted as supervisor of the Ft. Dauphin Mission Station and Inga taught French and other subjects in the girl's school. They returned to America and eventually settled in Everett, and then Seattle, Washington, where Gabriel worked as a Lutheran pastor and Inga taught confirmation classes and debate.

CHAPTER 3
CALLED TO MADAGASCAR

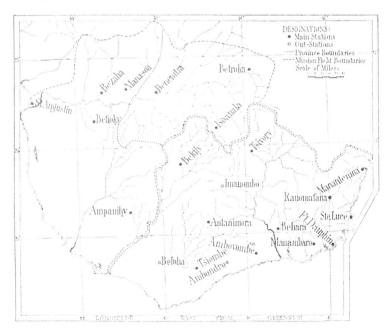 THE SCHOOL FOR BOYS WAS ORGANIZED SO THAT CHRISTIAN BOYS MIGHT BE EDUCATED AND TRAINED TO BECOME TEACHERS, EVANGE-LISTS, AND PASTORS.

In the year 1897 my husband and I were sent to Madagascar to be in charge of that institution.

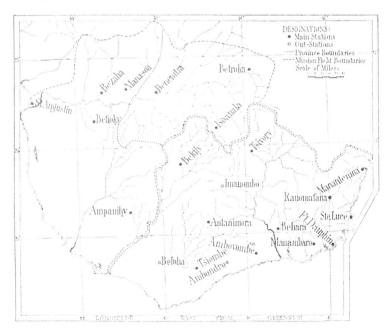

OUR SCHOOL FOR BOYS AT FT. DAUPHIN

The first work that my husband had to do was to supervise the building of a house for us. Building material had been shipped from Norway, brought by the mission ship *Paulus,* the sailing vessel that made its yearly voyage to bring missionaries to Africa and to Madagascar. In those days there were no sawmills to remodel the forest timber of Madagascar into building materials, so the Norwegian Mission [Society] found it necessary to send building material by ship. That was how stations near the coast got what they needed from Norway. Thus it was that our mission got materials for those houses

The home of Mr. and Mrs. P. C. Halvorson at Ft. Dauphin in 1898.

when our church took over the Ft. Dauphin district in the southern part of the island as our mission field. The Norwegian Mission Society had begun work there some time earlier. The house that now serves as the missionary residence was built by Rev. Hogstad.[27] My husband supervised the building of the second house. All the lumber was sawed and made ready in Norway. There were five rooms on the main floor, and a low attic. A veranda was built around the house. Mr. Halvorson did all the carpenter work, with several men to help him. He also built a church, topped by a small steeple. That was built of timber from the forest, which was beginning to come into use. Several men were sent to the forest to saw boards and planks, using hand saws. They were inexperienced and did not do a very good job, but what they managed to prepare was usable. Palm trunks were used to cover the walls on the inside, and they were

27. Rev. J. P. Hogstad was born in Trondhjem, Norway, and was a graduate of Augsburg Seminary in Minneapolis, Minnesota—a school founded in 1869 by Norwegian Lutherans who wanted to emphasize practical pastoral skills and missionary training over advanced study in theology and the liberal arts. He was sent to Madagascar by a Lutheran synod called the Conference of the Norwegian Lutheran Church of America, one of the forerunners of the American Lutheran Church (ALC), organized in 1960. Hogstad was sent by the conference, but his work was done under the auspices of the Norwegian Mission Society.

whitewashed.

The buildings of the school for boys were the school building, the dining hall, and the kitchen. Those buildings were erected according to Malagasy methods: the walls were built of palm tree trunks, and the roofs were covered with palm leaves, which is the custom near the coast.

On December 23, 1897, the school was opened, and there were 18 pupils. Several others came later. The parents were requested to accompany their boys to the school, and to promise that they would not

Lutheran church built by P. C. Halvorson in Ft. Dauphin in 1898.

take their boys out of the school before they had finished the course.

During the first four years, our attic served as a dormitory for the boys. Their number rose to above 60. All of them slept on the floor, as they were accustomed to doing in their homes. Large mats were spread on the floor, and each boy got a small blanket. They were not accustomed to using pillows, but I did make some small pillows for them, stuffing them with some dry flowers. It was not long before those pillows disappeared, and I think the boys gave them to their parents when they were home on visits. I came to the conclusion that they might as well get along without pillows, so I made no more of them.

The older boys were given work to do in spare moments. Two of them had the job of cleaning up the "dormitory" each morning, rolling up the mats, and sweeping the floor and the stairway leading down to the porch; two of them had the job of cleaning up the yard; and two others had the job of keeping the school rooms neat and tidy. Four of the older boys did the cooking. They worked at each job for a week, and then changed about. The meals were simple, usually such as they were accustomed to having in their homes. The main dish was rice. For dinner they had rice with fish or meat, and vegetables. Beans, sweet potatoes, etc., were usually served for supper. Bread, butter, milk, sugar, cake, and cookies they did not get, and they did not miss them.

Every beginner meets with difficulties, and so did those boys. The parents were very reluctant about entrusting their boys to the care of white people. It was not long until some Malagasy father came rushing to the school to take his boy home. We had many long debates with quarrelsome and unreasonable parents and grandparents, and quite often the result was that they took their boys home with them when they left. When the school was first opened, parents often came to visit their children and to see how they were being treated. When they learned that the older boys had a little work to do, they often spoke of them as "the white men's slaves." On several occasions they greeted us with these words: "We have come to visit your slaves." Mr. Halvorson would sometimes rebuke them: "If there are slaves here, we must be the ones, since we are struggling to educate and to clothe your children." Later they did not speak that way.[28]

The children certainly were far from easy to manage. They were accustomed to lying, stealing, and idleness. It caused us much anxiety and many hard struggles to lead and guide those youngsters along the way they should go. Much of faith, patience, and generosity were needed.

With God's help, conditions improved year by year. Many of those with whom we had to deal became new creatures—kind, obedient, anxious to learn, and capable, too. From that school for boys many teachers, evangelists, and pastors have come forth.

The younger boys were baptized as soon as we took them into the school. The older boys immediately began to prepare for baptism and confirmation.[29] Those who were baptized when first

28. P. C. Halvorson's salary as a Lutheran missionary in Madagascar was $900 per year. Peter's father, Christopher—a staunch supporter of mission work—helped Peter make ends meet by sending along money as he could. Christopher died in Sinai, South Dakota, in 1912.
29. In most denominations of the Lutheran church, infants are baptized shortly after birth as an expression of God's grace and biblical promises, but older children and adults receive catechetical instruction first, typically from a devotional pamphlet such as Martin Luther's *Small Catechism* (1529). Confirmation—a rite performed around the age of 14 in the 19th and 20th centuries—gave young adults who were baptized in infancy a liturgical opportunity to affirm the baptismal promises made on their behalf. Participation in the sacrament of Communion would typically follow soon after.

entering the school were between the ages of 6 and 11. There was no way of knowing their exact ages, for most of the parents kept no record of the years. One mother, when asked how old her son was, said that she thought he must be about a hundred years old. "It is a long time since he was born," she said. The boy was evidently about 11 years old.

Ft. Dauphin, with the early Lutheran church built by P. C. Halvorson in the distance. Several French flags fly in the breeze.

I was kept busy sewing clothes for the boys. When they entered the school, they had a filthy little cloth wrapped about them. We invested in many bundles of unbleached muslin, from which we made short shirts for their every day wear. I did have a little hand-machine, which was kept running early and late preparing clean clothes for the boys so that they might appear somewhat respectable. Then there was the problem of making Sunday clothes—a jacket, knee-pants, and a cap. Our assistant teacher, Rabenja, was clever at sewing with the machine, and he helped me when he was through with his classes. There were not many Malagasy folks at this station who were able to sew with machine, or even with a needle and thread, so I started a sewing class for a group of young women.

Well do I remember when our first 18 school boys got their Sunday togs on for the first time.[30] It was eight o'clock in the morning. They lined up, two by two, to march over to the church. How smiling and happy they were, and how proud! White caps and white clothes! Never before had they owned anything so beautiful, and I was as proud and happy as they were. We loved those boys, and they loved Papa Halvorson as if he were their own father.

30. Sunday togs: their finest clothing.

View of the Indian Ocean from Ft. Dauphin.

On Sunday afternoons, when the Sunday school was over, Teacher Rabenja, and often Mr. Halvorson, too, accompanied the boys on outings along the seacoast or through nearby woods, where the boys could pick wild berries and fruit. They certainly enjoyed those hikes. The smaller boys enjoyed rolling down the sand hills near the coast. That was their way of coasting down the hills. It was not so easy, however, to climb back through the deep sand. Mr. Halvorson usually stopped at villages along the way to call on sick folks and at different homes.

On Saturday mornings the boys went to a lake about two miles from town to wash their clothes and to bathe. They would return clean and radiantly happy. Our clothes were washed in that lake, too. Though they were washed in cold water, the sun bleached them and they turned out white and clean.

Mr. Halvorson taught the boys many games, too. At first they were not much interested in the games, feeling that they were so tiring. They preferred to get into some sunny corner, cover their heads with a cloth, and lie down to sleep. They would sleep until they were awakened, either to go to classes or to eat. A lazy habit that was, but after awhile they learned to enjoy playing games especially if Papa Halvorson was with them.

Our oldest son, Paul, was one of the first white children those boys had ever seen.[31] Often their relatives from the country came to

31. Paul Anton Halvorson (1898-1992) was born in Ft. Dauphin about a year after the missionary couple arrived in Madagascar. At Paul's birth, Antonette was 28 years old and Peter was 31 years old.

see Paul, and he had to come forth again and again so that some callers might get a good look at him. How they stared at that little boy with blue eyes and light hair. One was heard to say that the foreign boy must be quite old, since his hair was so white! Once a little girl from the school for girls burst into tears when she saw our white children, saying, "Oh, why didn't God make me white-skinned like these folks?"

One morning about six o'clock, a little boy came running up to us shouting: "Sakeos has fallen into the well!" Papa ran down the hill to where the well was. He had had the well dug, had boarded it up, and set up a ladder leading down to the water. None of the boys dared to go down into the well, so papa had to do it. The boy needed help, for he had cut his knee on the edge of the bucket which lay on the bottom of the well. He was taken to the hospital, where he had to remain for several weeks.

During the Christmas vacation that year papa and Teacher Rabenja accompanied the boys on a somewhat lengthy journey into the country, out to towns and villages where some of the boys had their homes. The boys had learned to sing well, and the Malagasy people enjoy singing very much. When papa and Rabenja conducted meetings at the different places, the boys sang. It was a joy to the parents to see how their boys had been developing. On one of those expeditions they were weather-bound in one of the towns in the forest. It rained several days in succession. The people up there in the forest did not have much in the way of provisions, making it out of the question to buy rice or other food supplies for so many. So Mr. Halvorson and the boys went out to a cactus bush, picked the fruit from that, and ate it. This cactus fruit is quite tasty and nourishing, too. Many of the natives live on that kind of fruit in times of drought and crop failures. In certain dry places, where grass was very scarce, the cattle often had to live on cactus leaves. People set fire to the dry grass and twigs around the cactus bushes to burn off the prickles. Cactus makes good, nourishing food for cattle, and it contains so much liquid that it serves as drink as well. There are certain localities in the Tandroy district where there is a scarcity of rain, and many of the people have to go a great distance to get water, so in cooking they usually place cactus leaves on the bottom of the kettles and sweet potatoes on top, and thus they need not use water to steam the potatoes.

Cactus bushes often served as hiding places for thieves and robbers. For that reason the French people did away with the cactus plants. They sent for insects that live mainly on cactus, and they put an end to those plants in about two years, to the great sorrow of the Malagasy people. It certainly was a great disappointment to have the cactus, which had been so plentiful as far back as any of them could remember, disappear so suddenly and so completely. Before long drought and famine swept over that district, and many of the people had to move away, and many died of starvation.

One of the older boys in school, Ferdinand, died suddenly. One Sunday he got permission to visit some of his friends in town, and had dinner with them. During the night he became very ill. Mr. Halvorson was with him and did everything that could be done for him, but he passed away before morning. The boys thought that he had been poisoned, and that might have been the case, for that was often practiced, especially when people were jealous of one another.

A fishing net was ordered for the boys. Since we were so near the sea—the Indian Ocean—there were ample opportunities to go fishing. Once or twice a week the boys planned to go out fishing after school, as long as the net lasted. The net was often torn by small sharks, and the boys had to repair it. That was a job they did not like, but if they were to go fishing, it had to be done. They would go down to the seacoast, chatting and shouting, as Malagasy boys usually do.

Our two little boys, Paul and Victor, joyously looked forward to those fishing expeditions.[32] The larger boys rowed out to lay the net, and when they hauled it in, all the boys took part. What fun it was for them to see so many fish—large ones and small ones—wriggling in the net. The fish were put into a sack and carried home,

32. Victor Norman Halvorson (1900-63) was also born in Ft. Dauphin and was two years younger than Paul.

Peter and Antonette with other missionary families in Madagascar (c. 1905). The Halvorson children in front are Victor, Frida, Paul. and Conrad.

with shouts and laughter. They feasted on fish for supper, and what they could not eat had to be smoked so that it would keep till the following day. There were no refrigerators or iceboxes.

The smaller boys enjoyed playing in the sand near the coast. Once, when our little boy, Victor, was about four years old, he was sitting near the seashore, his back turned towards the sea so that he did not see a huge wave that came rolling towards land. It rolled over him, and he was carried some distance down towards the sea. He lost his breath for a little while and then began to scream, but papa soon came to this assistance.

Once when we were walking along the coast with our children, white-capped waves were rolling up towards where we were. Victor shouted, "Mama, *Ronono betsaka!*" ("much milk"). He thought that it must be milk that was so white. Some time later he said, "Why do the waves come only to the land? Why don't they roll out into the sea, too?" "That is a question that wise folks can't answer," said Father.

One moonlight evening, when papa stood looking up at the stars, our little Paul uttered this warning, "Look out, Papa, so the stars don't fall into your eyes!"

One time when Paul stood looking up at a very high mountain—Bezavona—about four miles away from where we were, he said that if a ladder were raised from the top of that mountain, it ought to be possible to climb up to heaven and be with God. Oh, yes, the little tots have wonderful thoughts.

Difficult Problems Solved

The schoolboys always got meat for Sundays, which they cooked Saturday evenings in order to have it ready for Sunday dinners. Sometimes the meat disappeared and once both the meat and the kettle disappeared. It took some time before the thief was found. Alas, it proved to be one of our own hired helpers—a heathen whom we had recently hired to help in the kitchen, an errand boy. After a long trial he finally confessed, and promised to pay for what he had stolen, and that he did. The same boy had often pulled bunches of small onions out of my garden, taken them to the market place and sold them, keeping the money for himself.

We had a large compound, and boys could raise sweet potatoes, manioc, and peanuts. A good way for them to get exercise was to weed the garden, but a teacher had to be in charge of the work, otherwise it would not be done. Some of the boys owned a hen and some chicks of their own, and those they sold to get some cash for their own use.

One Sunday a mission-offering was to be taken up, so Robera, one of the schoolboys, sold his hen to Papa Halvorson, and gave what he got for it as an offering that Sunday. It certainly was generous of him to do that. They did enjoy giving, but they did not have much money to give.

Robera was a gifted boy. Mr. Halvorson was well aware of that, and thought that if he could stay on at school, he might develop into a great man. But Robera had a hot temper, and when he got on the outs with one or another of his schoolmates, he would run home. That he did on several occasions. The last time he ran away, Mr. Halvorson took the donkey, "Pickles," and rode out to Sonerana, the town where Robera's home was, several hours away. When he arrived at the home, Robera was not there. He had seen Mr. Halvorson approaching the place, and had run off to the woods. But Missionary Halvorson had decided not to go back to the school without him. The parents could do nothing to help find the boy, so the missionary stayed, conducted meetings, called at different homes, and did all that could be done to bring the Gospel message to those with whom he came in contact, continually praying that God would lead and guide so that the boy would return. On the

Peter Halvorson works with a group of Malagasy men, women, and children to process *Kasava* roots.

morning of the third day, Robera did come out of his hiding place.

"Let us go back," were the words with which he greeted Mr. Halvorson. It had been his intention not to return to the school, but suddenly he changed his mind. On the way back to school, he was given a chance to ride the donkey once in awhile, and that pleased him much. When they were back at the school, papa had a private conversation with the boy. Then he wrote the following words on a slip of paper: "I, Robera, will not run away from school any more, but will continue my studies till I have finished the course."

"Now," said papa, handing Robera the paper, "sign your name to this." At first the boy was not willing to sign his name, but finally he consented to do so.

Then papa said, "Now take it and put it in your Bible so that it may remind you of your promise."

Robera said later that that written promise was of great help to him when the evil spirit came upon him. He kept it in his pocket Testament, and he began to pray more fervently than he had done before, he said, and God helped him so that he continued at school and graduated. Later he worked as teacher and evangelist for several years. Then he attended the theological seminary, graduated, and was ordained together with several of his schoolmates: Johanesa, Oktav, Antoine, Albera, and others. That was after we had left for

Ordination service for three pastors in the church at Ft. Dauphin.

home. He sent us a good, long letter in which he said: "Now I am, through God's help and infinite mercy, ordained to the Holy Office, and shall proclaim the Gospel message to my own people. Next to God I have you, Papa Halvorson, to thank for that. Were it not for your kindness and patience with me, when I so often ran away from school, and had decided the last time I ran away, never again to return, this could not have been, but you did not give me up. You, yourself, came and kept waiting for me, and praying that God would give me a new mind, and God heard your prayers. Now I am so glad, so very happy. And now I am sending you that little piece of paper that you remember you gave me, that was of such great help to me, and yours is the honor and my gratitude for that."

Robera was a gifted and Spirit-filled pastor, and served for many years. He died a few years ago.

Jakoba taught a class in the Sunday school. One Sunday afternoon some of his friends from town came and wanted him to go out fishing with them, for the weather was just right for fishing. The boys had orders not to go out fishing on Sunday, but the temptation was too great for Jakoba. He got one of the other boys to take his class in Sunday school, and went with them. He threw his line out into the sea, and soon caught a small fish—an electric fish, they called it—one that could not be eaten. When he took it off the hook to throw it back into the sea, he cut his finger on a scale and dropped the fish. It fell on his feet and cut into the skin on both of them. The boy suddenly became very sick, and was not even able to walk up the hill, so two of the boys had to carry him. When they set him down, one of the boys ran up to the mission station to call Mr. Halvorson who was just then giving first aid to a man coming from another direction, who had been searching for oysters in some hollowed rocks, and had been bitten by a fish that practically tore the skin off his hand. Mr. Halvorson ran down the street to help Jakoba, who was screaming so that we could hear him a block away. He was suffering terrible pains and was almost gone when Papa Halvorson got to him. They carried him to the doctor, who immediately cooked some very strong coffee and gave him several cupfuls of it. His heart was on the point of stopping.

After Jakoba had recovered from that terrible attack, he said: "I had this coming, for I went without permission. I have learned a good lesson."

Esaia, another of our schoolboys, became a teacher and an evangelist. Every time he came to Ft. Dauphin, he dropped in to pay us a visit. "It is such a joy for me to come and look around here where I had my home for many years, and to be with you who were my parents and my teachers. The days that I spent here were the happiest days of my life, and I often thank God because I became a Christian and had a chance to get an education," he said.

Once when I asked him if he would not like to attend the theological seminary and become a pastor, he gave this reply:

"No, I am enjoying my work as teacher and evangelist so much."

A group of men at the evangelical school with Missionary Halvorson.

Alfred, another of the graduates from our school, served as a teacher for a short time, but he contracted tuberculosis and died. Among my memories of him, I have a little work of art—a rose in bloom—a free hand drawing, with the following request printed on it: "Remember me in your prayers." I don't know how he managed to get the paint. It was beautiful, and he certainly would have become a great artist if he had lived and specialized in art. He was especially gifted along that line.

Josefa Kely, or "Little Joseph," as we usually called him, was really the first boy that we had in our school. He was an outcast, the son of slaves. His mother died around the time when the slaves on Madagascar were set free, a short time after France had conquered the island as a colony.[33] The man who had owned the little boy did not want him when he was no longer counted as his property, and he was anxious to get rid of him. When the man went on an errand,

33. France completed its military conquest of Madagascar in 1895.

he put the boy in a calf-bin, for he had no one at home to look after him. The boy had not even begun to walk, but kept crawling about among the calves, though he was about three years old at the time. Because of lack of nourishing food, his legs were too weak to carry him. He was often badly in need of food and water. Sometimes someone would throw raw sweet potatoes into the bin to him. The calves had trampled on him, for he has large scars on this head to this day. Poor child! How he did suffer!

Then a couple of elderly Christians—a man and wife—heard about "Little Joseph." They immediately went to his master and asked if they might have him, and the man immediately gave his consent; he was glad to get rid of the child. The little boy had a good home for some time, but his foster-parents were elderly people and were planning to return to their home in the inland. They really were too old to take proper care of the child, and when they heard that we were to begin a school for boys, they brought him to us and to the school.

We hired a woman to take care of him, the wife of a man we had hired to get wood for the boys' kitchen. When the child was old enough to go to school, he joined the other boys. Once he contracted pneumonia and became very ill, so ill that we thought there was little hope for his recovery, but he did recover. Papa said: "God must have something special for him to do in this world." Some of the schoolboys said: "If Papa Halvorson is to be here all the time till Josefa Kely grows up and gets through school, then he will be with us here for a long time."

P. C. Halvorson with boys outside a modest Malagasy home.

A 25TH ANNIVERSARY CELEBRATION (1899-1924) OF THE MISSION SCHOOLS

Many of the boys from our school were later married to Christian girls who had been educated in our school for girls, and thus many Christian homes were founded, and thus the heathen were able to see the difference between Christian and heathen homes.

My sister, Caroline Nilsen, was the founder of the school for girls, and my brother, the Rev. Isolany, had charge of the mission station and the work in the congregation in the Ft. Dauphin district, after the Rev. Hogstad left. Mrs. Inga Isolany served in the capacity as teacher in the girls' school, also organist, singing instructor, sewing, etc., among student wives in the community. We, who were born in Madagascar, had been away for about 10 years before we returned to take up work there, but we had not forgotten the Malagasy language that we had learned when we were little tots. We often heard the people talking about how well we could speak their language. We could use their language as well as they themselves could use it.

The school for boys and the school for girls were begun about the same time, and July 10, 1924, the two schools came together to celebrate the 25th anniversary of their beginning.[34] The school for

Conference during the 25th anniversary, when many representatives of other missions were present, among them the mission secretary, M. Saeterlie.

34. Antonette describes two 25th-anniversary celebrations in this book: the 25th anniversary of the mission station in Ft. Dauphin (1889-1914) and the 25th anniversary of the two schools (c. 1899-1924). Chronologically, this second celebration is the last event she describes in the book. (Peter and Antonette returned to America for good in 1916.)

The 25th anniversary celebration of the Ft. Dauphin Mission in 1914.

boys had been moved into the country—about seven miles from Ft. Dauphin, to a place called Manantantely. There they had their celebration. The girls came from their school at Manafiafy to join in the celebration, a journey of about a day. They had a very festive program. Photographs were taken of the festive gathering and of the boys' music band, and sent to us. They also sent Papa Halvorson a gift in memory of what he had done for them. In a letter that they sent they said: "You taught us from the Bible, and because of that, we are sending you a Bible in the Malagasy language as a gift. We, your schoolboys, will always remember you and what you have done for us. We are so grateful because we were permitted to hear the gospel message, the Glad Tidings, and we thank you who brought us the message and taught us. We also thank fathers and mothers across the sea who sent you to us."

The girls also sent my sister, Caroline Nilsen, a special greeting and gift from their school. They loved her as they loved their own mothers, and many of those who had been her pupils named their children in memory of her.

"PICKLES"

Missionary Halvorson traveled about a great deal in the Ft. Dauphin district, and conducted Sunday services at many different places. He usually rode a donkey that had been named "Pickles." The animal had come from Arabia. After the French had conquered Madagascar, "Pickles" was sold by an officer, Rev. Isolany bought the animal for the mission, and it served us well for many years. "Pickles" was a good animal. He even served well as a church bell. Upon arriving in a village, "Pickles" usually brayed loudly so that people all over town could hear it, and then they knew that the missionary was there and that he came to conduct services in the church. When they returned to the main station on Sunday evenings, we could always tell when they had arrived, for "Pickles" would be sure to announce that.

"Pickles" had been raised in Arabia and was accustomed to climbing quite steep mountains. He would bend his front legs, get down on his knees, as it were, and, with the help of his long snout, he really was a master at climbing, but he was afraid of water, and dared not step into even a small puddle. He had to be led and blindfolded to cross a bridge.

"Pickles" was poisoned, by a witch doctor (we think). His death was really a heavy loss to us.

DOING AWAY WITH IDOLS

In one community where we began work (a small town, it really was), Missionary Halvorson gathered the people under some orange trees for devotion and for instruction. That was the first time those people had heard the Gospel message. Later, an evangelist was stationed at the place to carry on the work, and it prospered, as mission work usually does.

Malagasy *Ombiana*, or "idol priest," with many of the ritual components of traditional religion.

Protected Malagasy religious site with idols and oxen horns.

There was another outstation where an evangelist was working to spread the Gospel, but where there were very few who went to church, and very few children went to day school. An idol priest [*Ombiana*] was working among the people in that locality, and he gave strict orders to the people to keep their children away from our school, and the adults were forbidden to attend church services. Such a personality can often have great influence over heathen people, for they are easily frightened.

The heathen priest declared that the god he worshipped was greater and far more powerful than was the God worshipped by the white people. He also said: "If this Halvorson can shoot and hit my god, then I will believe in his god and worship Him." He felt perfectly sure that the god he worshipped could not be struck by a bullet, and he wanted Rev. Halvorson to try to see if it wasn't so. The evangelist wrote and told us about the matter, requesting that the missionary come the following Sunday, adding, "Bring your gun with you."

Mr. Halvorson did what he was asked to do. That Sunday morning he delivered a message to the few who had come to church. After the service he went out to the place where the idol priest had set up his god. He was followed by those who had attended the church service. Mr. Halvorson thought they had not heard about the challenge, but they had all been told about it, and were most anxious to see what the outcome would be. Some were praying in their hearts to the Almighty God, requesting that He would let the heathen see His power.

Mr. Halvorson said, when telling about the event, that his hands trembled when he took up the gun and aimed it at the idol.

The idol was a horn, or the tip of an ox-horn, hanging by a string that was attached to the top of a black post—a holy post—which was stuck into the ground (somewhat like a telephone post). A green leaf (also said to be holy) was wrapped around the horn so that it could not be seen. There it hung, dangling from the top of that pole.

Tanosy grave monument decorated with ox horns.

Mr. Halvorson took aim and fired a shot. The idol fell to the ground. That was evidently a great surprise to the idol priest. He picked it up, examined it, and cried, "It was hit! I shall throw it away; for now I am convinced! Now I shall worship Halvorson's God!" Rev. Halvorson had hit the small spot on the edge of the horn, which was not so hard and smooth— the only place where the bullet could have gone through that tiny piece of horn.

From that time on the mission work made rapid progress in that community. The idol priest became an inquirer and attended church regularly. The schoolhouse was also well filled, and "the Kingdom of God came to those people."

Rev. Halvorson picked up the horn that the heathen priest had thrown away, and placed it on top of a burden that a man (a heathen) was carrying, but the man put down the burden. He did not dare to carry it because of his heathenish superstition. A schoolboy, who was in the party, picked up the horn and carried it home. People asked him if he was not afraid to carry it, and he answered, "No, because I am a Christian." Rev. Halvorson wanted to keep that horn so that people at home could see what the heathen will worship.

Women's Missionary Federation

Ladies' Aid societies were organized in the different congregations, and the money gained through the sale of articles made by the women was also used towards the spreading of the Gospel message among the people in neighboring communities, placing and supporting evangelists in different localities to teach the inquirers. Thus the Ladies' Aid societies could share in the mission work.

We met one afternoon of each week—usually on Thursdays. The Malagasy women do not have much work to do in their homes, and it was easy enough for them to come together once a week. No refreshments were served. After devotions and the singing of a hymn, all of them began to work at their sewing. A committee had planned the work, purchased the cloth, and cut out garments for men and for women. Some carried with them their hand machines for sewing, and the work went on in full swing. Some did embroidery work, others crocheted. The things that they made were readily sold when the church people were gathered for conventions. People were anxious to buy ready-made garments in those days, for there were not many who could sew or who owned a sewing machine. We were also able to get small pieces of cloth (samples) from a merchant, and made patch-work quilts, using unbleached muslin as lining. The quilts were colorful and beautifully made. Everybody wanted them, so they were sold at good prices.

The word *bemiray* means "much put together." Some of the women often used those *bemiray* covers for *lamba* when they went to church. A *lamba* is a garment that Malagasy women use to throw over their shoulders, even though they wear pretty dresses.

Once each year the country congregations used to gather at the central church at Ft. Dauphin for a three-day meeting. The members of the congregations brought offerings—usually things to eat. These were auctioned off, and the money received was used for mission work. They brought baskets of rice, sweet potatoes, manioc roots, peanuts, beans, chickens, geese, ducks, and sugarcane. The schoolgirls also made donations, mainly of things that they had made. It certainly was encouraging to be present at those sales and to see how readily the things donated for the furtherance of God's Kingdom were purchased.

REVOLUTION

After France had conquered Madagascar and it had become a French colony, there was not actual peace in the land for many years.[35] Rumors of disorder and upheavals were reported from here and there, so that the government was obliged to adopt and enforce many laws to get the Malagasy people to become orderly.[36] As time went on the French people thought that the natives were fairly well subdued, and so the majority of the French soldiers on the island were sent home. Comparatively few of them remained, and they were stationed mainly in the larger cities, where Malagasy soldiers were also trained.

But the hatred that the Malagasy people bore against their conquerors was not quenched, and it burst out anew when they learned that so many of the French troops had been sent away from the island. "The time has come," said their leaders, "that we must rid our land of these white *Vazaha* who have taken possession of it!"

Then the revolution began, first in the interior, and soon spreading to the coast. The French government managed to check it

Malagasy warriors with traditional spears and "modern" flintlock rifles, c. 1905.

35. The French military conquest of Madagascar took place between December 1894 and October 1895. It was facilitated, in part, by a treaty England signed with France in 1890, which gave the French control over Madagascar in exchange for the English control of Zanzibar.
36. These laws included separate legal codes and penalties for the French and Malagasy peoples—a standard (and much despised) feature of many colonial systems in Africa.

for awhile but it wasn't long before it broke out again. Churches were torn down and burned. The rebels were planning to rid their country of missionaries, too, as well as of the French people, "for they are brethren," they said.

One English missionary, Rev. Johnson, together with his wife and a child, were killed, and the residence and the church at the station where they worked were burned. Their mission station was near the capital city. Two French missionaries who were on their way to a Norwegian convention at Betafo were shot as they passed a market place.

Once when the Norwegian missionaries were going to an annual convention at Fianarantsoa, they all took their families down to the Antsirabe station, for there was a military division at that place, and they thought they would be safer there than at the stations where they were working. The house at Antsirabe was a two-story building built of brick. Some French officers were there to protect them if the rebels should come. A band of rebels did come after they had burned a church and missionary residence at Loharano, about a three-hour march from there. The rebels had not expected to meet with opposition at Antsirabe, but things did not go so smoothly as they had expected. There were many rebels—about 1,400 men, we were told. The four French minor officers at the mission station were brave and able men, and they shot many of the rebels as they were approaching; but their supply of ammunition dwindled rapidly, and it would not have lasted many more days. The rebel gang was there for three days. Had not the church been built of brick, it would, of course, have been burned, as so many other buildings were. As the rebels were tearing down, breaking up, and chopping to pieces the pulpit and church benches, two persons of the besieged thought they heard someone shouting, "There they come! Don't you see the army coming from the south?"

The robbers must have heard the shout, too, for they immediately rushed out of the church and fled.

That night everything was quiet, so those who were besieged dared to go to the well out in the yard to get some water. The following day the rebels returned. They piled up straw and twigs around the house, mixing it with red pepper. Smoke from the pepper is terribly strong. But the moment they were about to set fire to the straw, someone caught sight of an army coming from the west. The army had been sent from Betafo to help those who were under siege. The rebels fled. God had again caused the rescue of His people!

The men missionaries who were at the convention were told that rebels were at the mission station to which they had brought their families, and one can well imagine how they must have felt. They hurriedly set out on their return trip, but it took several days to journey from Fianarantsoa. They met many refugees along the way, but no one had good news for them. "The rebels are besieging the station," was their report. On the last day of the return journey, however, they met a man who brought them the glad tidings that all their loved ones were safe and well. How they rejoiced. There was another proof of the fact that God was holding His protecting hand over His witnesses.

Then it was reported that the rebels were on their way to the coast, and were heading toward our Ft. Dauphin station. They murdered the people and burned homes, towns, and villages wherever they went, and did away with one military post after another, thus getting weapons and ammunition for themselves. There were many who joined up with them.

It was in the month of December 1904 that an awful rumor reached us. It became so still and quiet in the city. Many of the Malagasy people fled to the forests. We had to send our school boys back to their respective homes, after Rev. Halvorson had commended them into God's protecting care. Every one of those boys returned to the school after the revolution was over.

One Sunday evening, at dusk, as we stood looking towards Mt. Bezavona, we saw that a fire had been started at the foot of the mountain. The rebels were using that method of signaling their comrades, and here and there we saw other fires started as answering signals. We knew what it all meant, for rumors had informed us that the rebels were preparing to launch an attack. Later in the evening a message came from the captain, ordering us to go to the headquarters of the military forces as quickly as possible, for the rebel forces were approaching. Many of the Malagasy folks (old folks, women, and children) came and asked that they might stay in our house that night. They could not flee out of the city and thought that our house would not burn! Rev. Halvorson prepared a place for them in the upper story of the house (the boys were not there at the time), and commended them to the protecting care of God.

We left them there. One of them, a merchant, had taken with him a little box containing about $100 in silver, and asked Rev. Halvorson to kindly put it in a safe place. At the last moment, as we were about to hurry off, he did not know just what to do with it, and slipped it under a bed. The following day the man got the box back, and buried it somewhere, as their custom was, for there was no bank where they could deposit their money. The man had perfect confidence in Rev. Halvorson, though we knew little about him.

We had packed a trunk full of blankets, clothes, and some food supplies. This we managed to get with us. The station master, the Rev. M. J. Stolee, and family were there when we arrived at the military post. At this time we had four children—Paul, Victor, Frida, and Conrad. The youngest was only six months old.[37]

Victor and Paul Halvorson play with military toys, c.1904.

37. Frida Halvorson Olson (1902-90) and Conrad Nathan Halvorson (1904-74) were also born in Ft. Dauphin at the mission station.

We sat there all night, expecting the enemy to launch an attack at any moment. One of the boys, Victor, thought that we were at a festive gathering, for there were so many flags, and people were walking restlessly in and out all night long. It was late before he went to sleep. The children slept on the floor. The following day, when we made the trip home, Victor said to some of the Malagasy folks, "We were to a celebration last night!"

"No," said Paul, who is older and understood what was going on.

But Victor insisted that what he had said was true. "Didn't you see all the flags? Of course it was a celebration!"

It certainly was fortunate that the rebels did not arrive that night, for the old fort where we were was far from what it ought to have been. There were openings in the wall. The following day those were filled with sandbags, and broken bottles were strewn everywhere, for the rebels were barefooted. Only a few French soldiers were there. There were a few Malagasy soldiers, too, but if the rebels should launch an attack, they were not to be trusted.

Each night the women and children were crowded into a long, narrow room where soldiers used to sleep. There were a few small beds.

The men were out in the yard, for there was no house where they could lodge. Rev. Halvorson and others sat in their folding chairs night after night, with their umbrellas open; for there often fell light showers during the night.

Rev. G. Torvik, who was in charge of the Manafiafy station, had now moved to an island two miles from shore with his family and a lady teacher, because a rumor of an uprising arose. The rebels came shortly and destroyed everything in the station house. The captain at Ft. Dauphin sent a big boat to get them. This was the safest way, because it was uncertain to travel by land. However, it was very rough sailing along the coast line, and we were all very happy when they arrived safely in our midst. There was another close call, too, and that was Emma Dahl's flight from Manantenina. She left just in time because shortly afterwards the terrible rebels entered that station. Another demonstration of God's protection and mercy!

The French had captured two men whom they thought were agitating with the rebels. Those two men were finally shot, though many folks felt quite sure that they were innocent. One of them was the father of a boy attending our school, and we felt quite sure that he was innocent. Stolee and Halvorson asked the captain for permission to visit the two captives, to converse with them, and baptize them, if they so desired; but, no, they were not permitted even to speak to them.

During the day there were guards outside of the city for miles away, and those who wished to go to their homes to get food supplies could do so.

Our church bell, and that of the Catholic mission, were to be rung if there was anything suspicious going on, so that the people could flee to the fort, which was about half a mile from where we were. One day, at just about noon, our church bell began to ring, and immediately after that, the Catholic bell also began to ring. Everybody left what they had and fled. It was a false alarm, however. A woman had come from the market place, and, thinking that the rebels were there, had given a false report.

It took a long time before the rebels from the north were able to join up with those from the south. Then leaders met again and again. Finally they came to an agreement, and the rebels from the south decided to join up with those from the north in launching an attack on Ft. Dauphin, but they had to ask their idol priest, their oracle, to decide on a lucky day, and that, too, took time.[38] The day was finally decided upon. The rebel army had increased. There were many thousands of them. They must have food. A large number of animals were butchered. Meat and rice had to be cooked and prepared for the journey. Those who refused to join the rebel forces had to flee into the woods, otherwise they would be killed.

On the morning of the day on which the rebels had planned to launch their attack, a ship unexpectedly arrived. There was no way of sending mail or telegrams, for the rebels had chopped down the telegraph poles so that the white folks should not be able to send messages, and the mail carriers had been killed. Thus there was no way of communicating with people in other port cities. But in the city of Tamatave a bad rumor had been spread. It was reported that Ft. Dauphin had been attacked, and that all the white *Vazaha* had

38. For more on Malagasy traditional religion and the concepts of *vintana* ("luck" or "fate") and *ody* ("magic"), see P. C. Halvorson's historical essay below (Chapter 6).

been killed, and that their dead bodies had been strewn along the seashore. That was the reason the ship had been sent, and, near the harbor, the ship had been anchored for some time, signaling with flags. At first they thought rebels were signaling from shore, requesting that they land as soon as possible. But finally they caught sight of two white men walking along the shore, and the ship hurriedly entered the harbor. A number of Senegal soldiers, serving the French government, were put on shore. They prepared a meal for themselves before they set out for the place where the rebels were encamped.

They certainly sprang a surprise on the rebels who were just enjoying a festive meal preparatory to launching their attack on Ft. Dauphin. God sent His help at the last moment that time, too. We could not but thank God for the marvelous way in which He helped us. When it appeared most hopeless, then help was nearest.

At the time we were expecting the rebels to launch their attack at any moment, one Frenchman was walking around near the fort, very sad and downhearted "It does not matter so much about us older people," he said, "but when we have to see our children tortured and killed, how terrible!"

Rev. Halvorson then said: "Unless God permits it, that is not going to happen."

We were at the fort for 16 days. Our house which was outside the fort was filled with Malagasy people for 16 nights. They were crowded in like herrings in a barrel—all over the floors and under the beds. They did not use our beds. Our house boy was there, too, and looked after things. We did not miss so much as a needle. It would not have been difficult for any of them to have put some of our possessions under their clothes when they went back to their homes each morning, but they did not do that. They were in trouble, and, by doing wrong, they would get themselves into greater difficulties.[39]

39. Revolts against French rule would continue sporadically in Madagascar until France finally granted the island nation independence in 1960.

Chapter 4
Home on Furlough and Return

 The rebel-planned attack on Ft. Dauphin took place in December 1904. We went home on our first furlough in February, the following year. When we returned to the field for our second term, 1909, we were obliged to leave four of our children with relatives in the homeland, as there was no school for our missionaries'

Antonette holding Alida, who appears to be wearing a christening gown, in Ridgefield, Washington. Alida was baptized on January 1, 1906.

children on our Madagascar field at that time. That was arranged for later. Thus it fell to the lot of Madagascar missionaries to leave their children at home, mainly because they had to attend school. To leave the children behind when setting out for the mission field is far from pleasant for parents and for children.[40]

40. The four children were split among two families back in America. Paul, Victor, and Alida Florette Halvorson Mathison Brecke (1905-2000) stayed with Peter's twin brother Herman Halvorson (1866-1940) and his wife, Anna Boyd Halvorson, in South Dakota, while Frida was cared for by Antonette's relatives in Washington State. This breakup was later remembered as a difficult time for both parents and children. The youngest two, Conrad and Ruth, returned to Madagascar with Peter and Antonette.

Before the Halvorsons returned to Madagascar in 1909, they posed for a family portrait in South Dakota. Top (from left): Paul, Conrad, Ruth, Antonette, Peter, Alida, and Victor. Bottom: Since Frida had been left with relatives in Washington State (where she would remain for 10 years), it was necessary to paste a recent photo of her into the family portrait. In many respects, this image encapsulates the difficult choices missionary families had to make—and live with.

The mountain of Vesuvius as seen from Pompeii, Italy.

We had the opportunity of visiting many lands on the journey to and from our mission field, and that was most interesting, especially for Rev. Halvorson. Near Naples, Italy [on the way back to Madagascar], we visited the ruins of Pompeii, and other wonderful and interesting places. One day Rev. Halvorson took a train from Naples to the foot of Mt. Vesuvius, about seven miles inland, where he saw the ancient city of Herculaneum. He got a man to accompany him and ascended Mt. Vesuvius, riding on a donkey. The crater of the volcano, he said, was so huge that it must have covered several acres of land. He began to climb down into the crater to examine it more closely, but the guide called him back to inform him that many people had lost their lives that way, wanting to examine the crater more closely and had been overcome by gas. Rev. Halvorson went far enough down so that he began to smell gas and to feel that his knees were weakening. He heard a bubbling down in the crater that sounded like a huge kettle full of thick, boiling mush. He climbed up out of the crater safely.

The train on which he was returning was delayed that evening, and I and our two children, Conrad and Ruth, were at the hotel waiting for him to return. We began to be very anxious, fearing that he had met with some mishap. How happy we were when he finally joined us![41]

We were in England and in France twice, sailed around Africa—twice along the western coast, and twice along the eastern, through the Suez Canal and the Red Sea. Our journey through the Suez Canal took a whole day. When two ships meet there, one of them has to make room for the other and wait until it passes,

41. Mt. Vesuvius famously erupted on August 24, 79 A.D., and buried the Roman cities of Pompeii and Herculaneum with ash, stones, and mud, preserving the sites as virtually intact museums of the Roman Empire. Significant excavations of the cities began in the second half of the 19th century, and volcanic activity continues around Vesuvius to this day.

Top: The Halvorsons visiting the Nilsens near Battleground, Washington, c. 1906. Paul, Victor, and Frida are seated as Ommund and Herman split old-growth logs and two Nilsen women work a long saw.

Right: A light marker at sea.

because the canal is somewhat shallow. Every day a ship comes along and scoops up the sand at the edge of the canal. Sandbars move from place to place. It is not easy to travel that route; for it is very hot there, as well as along the Red Sea.

Once when sailing along the Red Sea, we saw a long stretch on one side of the ship where the water was red, and we came to the conclusion that that was how the sea got its name. At certain times of the year fish lay their eggs among the reeds and seaweed along the coast. Some of the seaweed are red, and when the sun shines, the sea appears to be red.

At Gibraltar our ship stopped for a whole day. The Rock of Gibraltar loomed up above us, perpendicularly. Everything that was to go up there had to be sent up by cable. The fortifications on all sides were full of holes for shooting through, all the way up to the top of the rock. On the side facing Spain, soldiers were on guard day and night, marching back and forth. There was a plain—a stretch of "no man's land"—about three miles between the Rock of Gibraltar and the nearby Spanish city, and on the Spanish side of that plain, Spanish soldiers were on guard. We took a ride over to the Spanish city, but did not enter the gate. The city is surrounded by a great wall, so high that we could not even see the city; but we heard a terrific noise, for they were having a bull fight there that day. Our guide told us that we must not enter the gate. "They will tear you to pieces, for they can see that you are strangers," he said. Mr. Halvorson did go up to the gate to look in, however, but he soon returned.

There was a great difference between that Spanish town and Gibraltar, where the British kept everything very quiet on the Sabbath.

HALVORSON RETURNS TO EVANGELIST SCHOOL

Rev. Halvorson was now to have charge of the school for evangelists. Many of those who had attended our school for boys continued their studies there, preparing to become evangelists and teachers in the service of the church. Many of them, after serving as evangelists for some years, attended the theological seminary and, after finishing the three-year course there, were ordained pastors. The Norwegian mission in the interior has a theological seminary in South Betsileo, Fianarantsoa, in which our mission also has a share.

The Norwegian, and our mission society, each has a teacher there.[42]

Missionary Eugene Rateaver instructed in band music, and we soon had a very good band.[43] Many of our students were members of it for several years. They were gifted, and eventually became very good musicians. We felt quite proud of them. Rateaver had studied at St.

An early graduation class at the evangelist school with Missionary Halvorson.

Olaf College, and specialized in band music. He was very highly esteemed among the Malagasy people, for they are very fond of music.

Mrs. Rateaver sewed uniforms for the band members, as the band was requested to play at important festivities, and especially on July 14 [Bastille Day], the national holiday of the French people. There were programs and various sports, and the country people gathered in town for the festivities. They listened to the music with deep appreciation.

Commenting on the work of the evangelist school in 1912, Missionary Halvorson wrote:

"It becomes more and more evident to me, as the years go by, that, if the Kingdom of God is to make such progress among these uncultured and superstitious people that the congregation can become self-supporting and mission work superfluous, then many of the people—yes, as many as possible of the people's own sons—must be educated and trained to become witnesses and messengers for Christ. The sooner that can be done, the sooner the congregation will become self-supporting.

"But, alas, we yet have far to go. It takes so long to get ripe fruit from the trees that are planted. To get able pupils, we must begin by

42. The two mission societies being discussed here are the Norwegian Mission Society and the Norwegian Lutheran Church in America (which eventually controlled the mission field around Ft. Dauphin).
43. Rev. Eugene A. Rateaver began his work at Ft. Dauphin in 1911, and spent his life working in the area for the Malagasy Lutheran Church. He is buried in the Ft. Dauphin missionary cemetery.

The Ft. Dauphin boys' school band, featuring Peter Halvorson (right).

getting the right kind of pupils. To get those takes a long time. The missionary must, as a rule, work for years, instructing in the Word of God, before the sons of these people show any willingness to be trained to become God's witnesses among their people. For that reason we do not get pupils from new districts or unworked mission fields. To train the pupils takes a long time—entirely too long a time, we think. But the darkness of ignorance is so dense, and superstition so deeply rooted that it often is more than fruitless to send young, spiritually frail students as workers among the heathen. And education makes little progress the first year or two. Superstition and heathenish ideas surround those young Christians like a filthy ice-covering, and it takes a long time ere the rays of truth can freely pierce through to their hearts and change them.

The first Malagasy pastors in the Ft. Dauphin mission field.

"The gifts for grasping and understanding are somewhat limited. If one imagines that some important truth has been pounded into their heads, he may discover, in a few days, that it has withered away. The lesson had not been fully understood. Abstract ideas are beyond their reach. Their mentality is, in that respect, like

Expanded station church built by Torvik to replace original Ft. Dauphin structure.

that of a child. Everything must be set before them in such a way that they can see and touch it. If you want to make clear to them the breaking of the First Commandment, and the result of that, then show them pictures from life and from the Scripture, for instance, the Israelites and the golden calf. If you want them to understand what love for our fellow men means, then show them the Good Samaritan. Thus all the instruction must be concentrated, as much as possible, and illustrated by pictures, if it is to be understood. That was the method that Jesus used, too, and we must keep that in mind in all our teaching and preaching, in order to succeed.

"If we find difficulty in getting the truth into the brains of the majority of our pupils, we will find it doubly so to get it into their hearts. They are the sons of their ancestors. The heathenism and vice that surrounded them in their homes have influenced their characters so that it takes us a long time to patch them up and straighten them out. We teach, admonish, and punish. We try to influence them by love and by being strict with them. That is necessary, but does not help much. Their hearts are continually hardened. As time goes on, however, one perceives that the leaven of the Gospel has wrought great changes. The darkness begins to pass away, superstition weakens, and the mind becomes more and more controllable. A worker is being developed: quietly, and little by little he ripens and becomes a noble servant in the Master's vineyard. Oh, how encouraging it is to see that! It helps when struggling on with the seemingly hopeless ones, and to be patient with those who are perverse.

"We have seen great progress in Christianity among our pupils this year, especially among those of the upper class. Many of them are strong and courageous young men. May God help them to continue growing in faith, hope, courage, and endurance!

"The state of health has not been the best this year. Many have suffered from fever. Four children and one woman have passed away this year. The woman contracted lockjaw—tetanus. That is very common here. Though everything possible was done for her, there was no hope for her recovery. Between the attacks she felt quite well and told about wonderful visions of Heaven that she had had. The saved were dressed in white, and Jesus was standing among them. She could easily recognize Him. 'Now that I have seen how happy they are, I am not longing to recover,' she said.

Ruth Halvorson with a local Christian who also served as Ruth's wet nurse.

"After one of the attacks, her relatives thought that she was dead, and began to weep. When she came to and saw that they were weeping, she said, 'Why are you weeping?' 'We thought you were dead,' was the answer. 'Yes, I was almost dead, but I asked Jesus to let me come back to you so that I could admonish you,' she said. Then she turned to her father and said, 'I did not see you among the saved, and that has saddened me so. If you want to see me again, then you must do as I do believe in Jesus. What the missionaries tell about God is true.' Then she embraced her parents and her children and said, 'I love you so, but you must follow me; for it is so glorious in Heaven, and it is not so far away as people think. It is near by.'

"Often she admonished her relatives and friends, and at last she bade goodbye to each one of them. Finally she said, 'There is Jesus, waiting for me. Oh Jesus, receive me! I am coming home to you!' She heaved a sigh, and her soul left the body. She had gone to the Heavenly Home.

"Her blessed departure made a deep impression on all. 'We've never seen anything like that before,' said some of her heathen relatives. Her father, who, at that time was a fallen Christian—an idol worshiper—permitted no liquor to be used or heathenish customs practiced at her funeral; and he told the people about her blessed departure.

"The above mentioned woman was the wife of one of our pupils at the Evangelist School and she had been educated at our girls' school."

CHAPTER 5
RETURN TO AMERICA

IN 1916 WE WENT HOME ON OUR SECOND FURLOUGH. THAT WAS
AT THE TIME OF THE FIRST WORLD WAR. We were obliged to
cross over to Africa in order to board ships that would take us to
England.[44] After waiting there for three weeks to secure passage, we
were told that the ship we were to go on was heavily loaded with
gold that was going to England and that it would be a dangerous
journey, for submarines might launch attacks, but the ship was very
speedy and we got through safely. A couple of times, something that
looked dangerous came into view, but, by the help of God, we got
through. When we were near the coast of France we seemed to have
had a narrow escape. The ship sailed on with very dull lights at
night. That night there was still less light, but we sped on more
rapidly than usual. Many of us passengers—Norwegian and Swedish
missionaries—gathered down in the dining room for prayer meetings after the evening meal. That night the steward came down, put
out the lights, and covered the windows. Then we realized that
something dangerous had been seen. The captain gave orders that
all who had children must sleep on deck that night, and that the
children were to sleep with their lifebelts on. The adults must have
their lifebelts hanging on deck chairs and within easy reach.

44. The boat left from Durban, a port town on the east coast of South Africa. This time,
the boat apparently traveled back to Europe along the west coast of Africa.

However, we were not especially frightened or worried. We knew that it was God who ruled.

After a sea voyage of three weeks, from Durban, Africa, we arrived safely at Plymouth, on the southern coast of England, where all the British passengers went on shore. We Americans, Norwegians, and Swedes asked for permission to go on shore, too, but that was not granted. We were to stay on board the ship till we reached London. We sailed along the English Channel for three days, waiting for the fog to lift when the ports along the coast could be opened. There the ship might have been fired upon. We heard shooting continually. Heavy fog covered us, especially in the forenoons, so that we could scarcely see ships that lay quite close to us, and for that reason, every ship had to ring a large bell every three or five minutes in order to prevent collision.

On the third day at about one o'clock in the afternoon, the fog had disappeared and the different ports were opened so that the delayed ships could set out. It was a beautiful sight. More than 50 ships were headed for London, some moving along more rapidly than others. One ship passed so close to ours that we almost had a collision. Some of the ships were partly wrecked, and were moving along very slowly, leaning to one side, and some had broken masts.

Arriving in London, we stayed at a hotel for a few days. Missionary Pedersen and family were among our traveling companions. We were told that the first bomb that fell in London struck the hotel that we were in, but it did not explode. It had frightened the people there terribly so that they had fled to the streets.

We continued our journey by train as far as Liverpool, and there we boarded a ship that was on its way to New York.

Several years later, our son, Conrad, went to Madagascar (1932). For some years he was in charge of the school that his father had begun. But the school had grown much larger and had been moved out into the country, to a place called Manantantely, about seven miles from Ft. Dauphin.

Keepsake photos from the Halvorson home in Ft. Dauphin, featuring Peter's parents on the left and Antonette's parents on the right.

We have two little graves at Ft. Dauphin. Our children, Anna and Herman, died when they were quite young.[45] The rest of the children—Paul, Victor, Frida, Alida, Ruth, and Olaf—are here in the United States.[46]

My husband longed to return to Madagascar to continue the work that he so dearly loved, but his health did not permit him to do that, and so for many years, his work was mainly traveling among congregations here in the homeland to speak on missions and to show pictures that he had taken when we were out on the mission field. These seemed to be of great interest and to awaken love for mission work. Though those journeys often were long and tiresome, he was always happy and elated when he returned home.

---

45. Antonette lost two girls named Anna and two boys named Herman to childhood deaths in Madagascar. Antonette's sister Anna Olivia Nilsen died from malaria in 1886, and Antonette's infant brother Herman Adolf Nilsen died about 1880. (A second brother named Herman Adolf would later survive.) Anna Olivia Halvorson, Peter and Antonette's first child, was born at Ft. Dauphin on July 11, 1897, but died a week later on July 18. Herman Halvorson was stillborn, or died shortly after birth, on January 13, 1910.
46. Vital statistics for the Halvorson children are as follows: Paul Anton Halvorson (1898-1992), Victor Norman Halvorson (1900-63), Frida Halvorson Olson (1902-90), Conrad Nathan Halvorson (1904-74), Alida Florette Halvorson Mathison Brecke (1905-2000), Ruth Halvorson Berge (1907-96), Olaf Halvorson (1913-1952). The Halvorson children are survived by many children, grandchildren, and great-grandchildren in America.

Halvorson family reunion about 1920, featuring Alice, Arthur, Juliet, Paul, Constance, Clifford, Lillian, Victor, Frida, Gabriel, Inga, Peter, Antonette, Herman, Anna, Arnold, Conrad, Olaf, Ruth, and Alida.

It was his aim in life to spread the Gospel and to awaken mission-interest among his fellow men.

Nine months after Rev. Halvorson had ceased making those missionary journeys, he died suddenly of heart failure. He went out to get some wood for the stove and was found later in a praying position kneeling on a block of wood. That happened September 27, 1937.

In closing this account of bygone days, I wish to say this: God's hand has protected and kept us on all our sojourns in so many marvelous ways. Thanks be to our Heavenly Father!

"Bless Jehovah, O my soul; and all that is within me, bless his holy name. Bless Jehovah, O my soul, and forget not all his benefits."
(Psalm 103:1, 2)

PART II

REFLECTIONS ON MISSIONARY ACTIVITY
IN MADAGASCAR

CHAPTER 6
A BRIEF HISTORY OF THE MADAGASCAR MISSION, 1888 – 1913

BY PETER C. HALVORSON

 THE FIELD

IN THE SOUTHEASTERN CORNER OF MADAGASCAR LIES THE PROV-
INCE OF FT. DAUPHIN.[47] It is bounded on the north by the provinces of
Farafangana and Betroka, on the west by the province of Tulear, and
on the east and south by the Indian Ocean. The size is approxi-
mately 23,000 square miles, and it is divided into two main parts—
Anosy in the eastern part, and Androy in the western.

The landscape varies throughout the different parts. The large
mountain range that stretches from Cape Amber in the north to
Andrahomana in the south separates the east coast from the highlands, and also Anosy and Androy, thus dividing the province into
two entirely different parts. In the eastern and northern parts there
are high, jagged mountains with deep valleys cut through by creeks
and rivers.

As the landscape varies, so does the climate. Among the
wooded mountains and deep valleys in the eastern part there is
much rain and splendid vegetation. In the valleys and down by the
coast are ill-smelling marshes full of rotting plants—a paradise for
mosquitoes and other insects. The air is moist and the heat oppres-

---

47. This essay was apparently prepared as part of the 25th anniversary celebration of the
Ft. Dauphin Mission Station. Its formal headings indicate that it was also designed to
serve as a status report on the state of the Ft. Dauphin mission field.

sive. The western part is extremely hot and there is little or no rain. The air is dry and pleasant. The heat is very oppressive, especially in the summer, so much so that it is positively danger-ous to the health. That people from the north can endure living there is due to the cool nights. Even during the worst heat the nights are cool and pleasant. The most common climatic diseases are malaria and dysentery. The first mentioned is really the most common, but the

Two Malagasy work near a "Traveler's Palm."

second is the most dangerous. Though Ft. Dauphin is a little off the tropics, the climate is tropical in every way. Besides the regular tropical diseases that attack both natives and Europeans, the latter often suffer from headache and sunstroke because of the strong sunshine and heat.

THE PEOPLE

The province of Ft. Dauphin is the mission field of the United Lutheran Church.[48] According to the census of 1912, the natives number 223,208, but they could not all have been included in that, so the number could be raised to 250,000. About 150,000 are of the Tandroy tribe, 50,000 of the Tanosy tribe, 9,000 of the Tatsimo tribe, 8,000 of the Tambolo tribe, and the rest are mixed. As to appear-ance, they are much alike. They are a tall, well-built people of color varying from light brown to almost black. They are supposed to be of the Malay, or yellow race, but they are mixed with the black race, most likely from Africa. The tribes differ in language, manners, and

48. The United Norwegian Lutheran Church in America merged with two other Norwegian Lutheran synods in 1917 and became the Norwegian Lutheran Church of America, a predecessor body of the America Lutheran Church (1960) and the Evangelical Lutheran Church in America (1987).

customs. The original language is the same, but each tribe has its own dialect. Their homes are mostly of a primitive kind—small huts, from 6 to 10 feet square, built of wooden poles with roofs and walls of palm leaves or grass, depending on which is more easy to get. The entire family lives in that kind of hut. There they cook, sleep, and eat. It is quite evident that cleanliness is far from common in those homes, even though the people have some faint ideas as to what cleanliness is. Fortunately the huts are so flimsy that both the sun and the wind can enter and disinfect them.

Like children of nature at the most primitive stage, they have very few necessities, and the climate does not demand much of them either. Those who have not, as yet, been touched by civilization dress as Adam did, using a small strip of cloth instead of fig leaves, while those who have learned civilized customs use the *lamba*, a long piece of cloth that they throw over their shoulders. That serves as clothing both night and day.

Providing for "daily bread" is not a custom familiar to them. The land is fruitful, and the people do not suffer, as many civilized people do, from dyspepsia or poor digestion. Thus they are able to get what little they need by a minimum of work. They putter around at planting rice, corn, and various vegetables, and that supplies all they need in the line of food. Since the climate is warm the year around, there is no set time for planting and for harvesting, but they watch for the time of the year when the different plants seem to thrive best. The work of planting and harvesting usually falls to the women. The men prepare the fields and look after the cattle. Raising cattle is practiced on quite a large scale, and that is the main source of wealth for the Malagasy people. It can, however, scarcely be considered a livelihood; for cattle raising is carried on mainly because it has a part in Malagasy society and cult. In later years, though, it has become a branch of their livelihood; for hides are being shipped from the province, bringing in about a quarter of a million dollars a year. It was not to the liking of the Malagasy people that they were not permitted to eat the hides, as their custom has been. It was the French government that forced them to sell the hides. Besides farming and cattle raising, they also do other kinds of work, such as fishing along the coast, getting rubber from the

A tribal meeting under the trees, with Peter Halvorson preaching (left).

forests, raising bees, chickens, etc.

Their social life is patriarchal. An old grandfather who might have had many wives gathers about him his children and grandchildren with their families. Those in turn may have entered "blood-brotherhood" with other families, and thus are formed "house-groups," as they call them. The towns are usually well fortified by cactus hedges that cannot be broken through by either men or beasts. A narrow path, often very crooked, leads up to an opening in the hedge. That is the only entrance to the town, and it is carefully closed in the evenings after the cattle have been driven in. Those well fortified towns were a necessity for protection against thieves and robbers before the French became rulers of the island; for it was the greatest joy of the Malagasy heathen to rob their fellow citizens of cattle and women. Now conditions have changed, for thieves are severely punished, and it is difficult for them to escape; but proofs of the fact that the nature of the people still frequently rises above the training are the many bands of chained prisoners that are taken to the prison colony on St. Marie. They still do not value human lives when stealing cattle.

Marriages are loosely knit together and easily untied. In the most difficult cases, an ox or two might be used to settle the problems. The children (if there are any) belong to the man. That gives some idea as to the general position of women. A woman has no rights. Children they prize highly, especially boys; and even if a man chases his wife away, the children belong to him. And if the wife runs away from the man, lives with another man and has children, those children also belong to her first husband. The children receive no training, except to fear their fathers and to bend before fate.

Elephants are not native to Madagascar, and this elephant (photographed by P. C. Halvorson) is of Asian, not African, origin. It may have been brought to the island as a source of labor.

Any kind of punishment is not to be spoken of. They must learn to win over their parents so that they soon might be able to win over others as well. By nature they are quick and usually have good memories. It is fairly easy for them to grasp ideas and to keep them; but they are lacking in initiative.

Religious Conditions

The need for religion is deeply rooted in human hearts, and is found in the most primitive people. Thoughts and conceptions about our existence may differ widely, and there may also be differing opinions as to life hereafter, but the desire to seek help and guidance for what lies beyond and above one's self is common to all, and a proof of the fact that human beings cannot be self-sufficient. The many groping attempts made by people down through the ages in order to satisfy that longing, attempts that, among primitive people, have resulted in shameful idol worship, and among civilized people, entangled religious systems, are a proof of the fact that there is something about human beings that does not find full satisfaction in materialism. The lost vision of God is not completely erased from human hearts. The Malagasy people also furnish proofs of that. There are tribes (among others, the Tandroy) on our mission field that still have no sign of civilization or culture, and consequently are in the primitive stage in the history of mankind. And still, it can be said of them that they are a religious people.

Common to all the Malagasy people is the belief that there is only one god, whom they call *Zanahary, Andriananahory,* or *Andriamanitra.* The first two names translated mean "Creator"; the third, "The Fragrant Nobleman." The first one they fear, for he is supposed to have power over life and death, and it is of vast importance for them to keep on good terms with him. Judging by the name *Andriamanitra,* they must know him from the good point of view. That, however, is not really true. They do not know God, and because of that, they have taken upon themselves to "worship the creature instead of the Creator." National cultural worship does not exist in Madagascar. The people are divided into tribes, and, though they have much in common, they differ widely in many respects. The worship of ancestors might be said to be a national trait, but it is practiced in different ways in the different tribes, and thus it cannot be said to be a national trait.

Ancestral worship is, however, the main religion of the Malagasy people. Their need for religion seemed unable to express itself in anything higher, and fear (not love) is what spurs them on in their worship. To violate the commandments and the decrees in ancestral worship is unpardonable, and can be forgiven only through the sacrifice of animals, especially oxen, and the commandments of the ancestors are many. They have to do with every step "from the cradle to the grave." At birth, circumcision, marriage, sickness, death, burial, and various other events, *Ombiana,* an idol priest, or a witch doctor who through witchcraft and *sikidy* (a kind of witchcraft), decides what is to be offered up—killed. There are many ceremonies connected with such events, and it will be too difficult to go into further details now. This might be mentioned, however. No sacrifice is considered too great (if the family is able to furnish it) and without a murmur from those involved, the fattest of oxen and the best in the herd is offered. The idol priest is considered a sort of representative for the ancestors and for the higher powers, and the rascals (as they usually are) understand how to swing the whip over the consciences of the people.

The *Helo* worship belongs to another class. That is probably not so wide-spread, and is practiced more at certain places. *Helo* (the evil one, or evil power) is supposed to be located at certain places, and has certain *ombiasas* (priests or priestesses). He has great power and is able to bring on many kinds of misfortunes, make people sick and dumb, and can even kill them. It is therefore necessary for the people to keep him away by offering sacrifices and by giving gifts to his *ombiasa.* He is, in all cases, an enemy, and nothing good can be expected of him. The best thing to do is to get him to keep away.

A near relative to *Helo* is *Bilo.* He has no special place of abode, but enters into human beings and makes them sick. Practically all kind of sickness come about through "*Bilo*-possession," and, for that reason, it is important to cast out *Bilo.* That is accomplished through singing, dancing, and the butchering of oxen with many ceremonies that may last for a week or two.

The people are bound by many forms of superstition besides those mentioned here. There are *Mpamosavy* ("sorcerers") who can bring all manner of misfortunes on

Tanosy grave monument protected by oxen horns.

people through witchcraft. They are wicked and revengeful, and able to kill people by means of their witchcraft. That they make use of poisoning in their terrible evil-doings which they always practice in secret is quite evident, but they are protected by superstition. They are both feared and hated. If a *Mpamosavy* were caught in the act of evil-doing, he would have to "run the gauntlet" through the town, and then be killed and burned.

Among the good wizards are rain-makers. Others are supposed to control thunder and lightning; and still others are supposed to be in possession of means by which they can prevent grain from being destroyed by grasshoppers, etc. All of these have their *ody*—magic means or medicine. The medicines that they, through experience, have learned to know about and prepare from different kinds of plants and roots, might be helpful, but the magic is, of course, sheer nonsense, based on the superstition of the people. In connection with witchcraft is the choice of lucky days and warnings. Every month and every day of the month is supposed to be of some special importance, and woe to the one who begins his work or undertakes to do something that he should not do on an unlucky day. Before every important undertaking, the *sikidy* must be questioned. If *vintana* ("luck" or "fate") is good, the work might be begun; but no one dares to undertake doing anything special on an unlucky day. Choice of days has been the cause of many kinds of cruelty, but it is especially tragic for newborn babes. Though Malagasy people love their children with true, earnest love, they cannot save them if they are born on a very unlucky day. Then they must be thrown out, buried alive, or be killed in some other way. If the day is less unlucky, the babe's life might be ransomed through offerings, and it is the *ombiasa* (the witch doctor) who, by means of his *sikidy*, makes the decision.

This was the condition of the people before Christianity was introduced; suffering bodily from sickness and witchcraft; suffering spiritual torture because of bad conscience and superstition, and haunted by evil spirits—"without God and without hope."

POLITICAL CONDITIONS

From family to tribe, from tribe to nation, such is the history of a people, and the natives of Madagascar are no exception.

On the lofty plain, at the foot of the Ankaratra Mountains, about 5,000 feet above sea level, lives the most intelligent tribe on the island—the Hovaites.[49] Toward the close of the 18th century, their king, Andrianampoinimerina, began to enlarge his kingdom, subduing the tribes that were nearest. His descendants continued the enlarging policy until they, at the end of the 19th century, had conquered nominally the entire island. There were, however, many tribes in the outskirts of the plain that they never succeeded in conquering, though they did occupy several towns belonging to those tribes, namely: Ft. Dauphin, Tulear, and others.

---

49. Most historical sources call this tribe the Merina.

Andrianampoinimerina's plan to unite the tribes was good, and it might have saved the Malagasy people politically if it had continued according to his planning, but, unfortunately, the Hova tribe lacked the necessary foundation on which national unity can be built and continue—truth and justice. They showed pride and haughtiness in their dealing with the other tribes, and treated them cruelly and unjustly. Even the members of their own tribe dared not trust one another. Their government was corrupt and could not have continued had not another government come into power and created a political rebirth. Such a power began to enter the land when the London Missionary Society started their mission work on Madagascar in 1818, and other missionary societies followed. But the Christian ideas did not have time to leaven either the rules or the people. If the spirit of the martyr church of centuries previous could have worked, the church would have been able to save Madagascar for the Malagasy people. The fire that Queen Ranavalona tried her best to quench, even with the blood of martyrs, was quenched by billows of mass-conversions—mainly nominal, alas.

Madagascar had its "Harald the Fairhaired," but not a St. Olaf or Sverre Sigurdson, and, though the plan of Andrianampoinimerina, to gather all the tribes of the island into one kingdom, was carried out nominally, those who came after him were lacking in power to carry on to victory. For that reason their country had to fall prey to foreign powers sooner or later.[50]

If the government in the capital and vicinity was rotten, it was, of course, no better in the different provinces, where, because of poor communications, it was difficult for the central government to have much of effective control over the officers, even though there might have been some desire to do so. Every petty officer could carry on according to his own desire. If he were ordered to go to the capital, on one or another occasion, to be reprimanded, he usually managed to find some way of getting out of it, for he had powerful friends at the court, as a rule. Otherwise he might use money to buy

50. Peter Halvorson's description of the ineptitude of Malagasy government is not entirely consistent with Antonette Halvorson's firsthand assessment of Queen Ranavalona III and her prime minister in Chapter 1. The fact that England and France were both pressing hard to annex Madagascar as a colony in the late 19th century should be seen as the primary reason for Madagascar's political and military downfall.

III

himself out of it. They always knew how to make money when they were in office.

The province of Ft. Dauphin, one of those farthest away from the capital, never did get under the Hova rule, except nominally. They did occupy Ft. Dauphin and vicinity, but dared not venture into the western cities of Tanosy and Androy. Petty kings were the rulers there, and these continued to carry on as they had done in the past. They took pleasure in robbing cattle and women from their neighbors. If soldiers from the nominal capital dared to venture too far into the interior, they were driven back with "bloody brows." And the Hova could not stand the climate down by the sea. There was much sickness among them, and many died of fever and dysentery. But in Ft. Dauphin and vicinity the Tanosy people were made slaves, and the rulers over them led most reckless lives, drinking and practicing all kind of bad customs, and that in spite of the fact that they were supposed to be Christians from Tananarive! There it was considered stylish to be a Protestant, for the queen and her entire court were Protestants. Christianity had become the official religion of the land, and the Hovas had planned, besides conquering the entire island and uniting the Malagasy people politically, to introduce Christianity among the heathen tribes, when they began to rule over them. That the conquered people were forced by their conquerors to accept Christianity has been, in all cases, most unfortunate because of the subdued hatred that the conquered people have for their conquerors. And it becomes doubly unfortunate when forced upon them by "cultured" evil-doers whose morality is even below that of the heathens. That the queen and many of the leading men were earnest Christians is not to be doubted; but the majority of the people, even though nominally Christians, were liberated heathens. They had lost faith in their "old gods," but had not learned to believe in the "only true God." Thus they were free to follow their own unbounded passions, without faith, and without respect for what is holy. But nominal Christians they were, and eager to spread Christianity through ordinances and by attending divine services. The heathen tribes that knew nothing about Christianity and judged mainly from what their rulers practiced, could not but conceive hate towards a religion, the followers of which trampled under foot what they regarded as holy, treated the conquered people brutally, and, in private life, appeared, in many cases, to be even worse than the heathens. There may have been honorable exceptions, but even among the leaders of the highest rank there were unscrupulous rascals.

In 1889, Ramananjo, an officer of the 12th degree of honor (the highest degree that could be obtained was 15), was sent to Ft. Dauphin as governor. He was a Christian Protestant and was very eager to spread Christianity. He forced the people to go to church, to keep from working on Sundays, to send their children to school, etc. He went to church regularly, and often took part in the services. That, however, did not prevent him from living sinfully in many ways. He was very miserly. That led him to commit a sin that might be looked upon as sacrilegious. He opened some old royal tombs, and stole jewels of silver and gold that he found there. So shameful a form of robbery had not even been heard of before, and rumors about it were spread abroad even in the capital city, and the minister of war, Prince Ramahatra, was sent down to investigate matters and to discharge Ramananjo if he should find the report to be true. Ramananjo dared not wait for the arrival of the prince, however. He committed suicide.

Such, then, was the general condition here in the middle of the fourth quarter of the last century. The province of Ft. Dauphin with its quarter of a million citizens was divided among several tribes that nominally were under the rule of the main tribe, but, in reality, it was independent. It continued to be, as it had been through centuries—a sunny land with its dark-skinned inhabitants tied up in the worship of ancestors and in superstition, torn by wars between different tribes, and very unsafe because of the many robber bands that roamed about and camped in the forests. But it is a land with great possibilities, when the people finally are liberated from their lengthy slavery and the chief of darkness is forced to flee before "the white Christ."

THE FOUNDATION OF THE MISSION

Some attempts, on the part of the Catholic Church, to introduce Christianity among the Tanosy people was practically fruitless, as their teachings had disappeared completely from the heathendom. Their pupils, too, if there ever were any, had disappeared. It was the Hova people who, in their struggle to conquer the entire island, during the latter half of the last century, first brought

DR. MARTIN LUTHER

Portrait of Martin Luther from the study of P. C. Halvorson.

the Gospel message to Ft. Dauphin. Most of them had been pupils of the London Missionary Society in Tananarive. That they were sadly unfitted to bring the gospel to the heathen tribes as previously mentioned, does not reflect on the church to which they belonged, but was due to the nature of the leading tribe—unreliability and pride. The majority of them were not truly converted Christians, but had accepted Christianity because it was the religion of the court and of the state. The new teachings made no progress among the Tanosy people, and they did not make efforts to spread it abroad. They had Sunday services and Sunday school for those in office, soldiers, and colonists—Hovaites or other tribe members.

In 1880 a couple of evangelists were sent from the capital, but they worked only among their own people. One or another of the Tanosy might, through curiosity, or, if forced to do so attend church services or Sunday school now and then, but there was no spreading of the Gospel among the Tanosy people.

In the meantime the Norwegian Mission Society had been looking towards South Madagascar. It had, long ago, begun work at Tulear, on the west coast, and looked upon all of South Madagascar as its mission field. In 1887 a Norwegian missionary—Rev. Nilsen-Lund—journeyed across the island from Tulear to Ft. Dauphin to examine the field. In those days such a journey was both difficult

19th century engraving of Luther's trial before Charles V at the Diet of Worms (1521), also from P. C. Halvorson's collection. Luther's heroic stance has long been an inspiration for Lutheran pastors in the field.

and dangerous; but the early Norwegian pioneers of the mission did not fear the dangers or give up because of difficulties. Through the merciful protection of God he got through safely, and the following year Ft. Dauphin got its first white missionary. That was Rev. J. P. Hogstad, born at Trondhjem, Norway, a graduate of Augsburg Seminary, Minneapolis, Minnesota, and sent out by the Conference of the Norwegian Lutheran Church of America. Since the church did not have a mission field of its own, and was supporting the Norwegian Mission Society, Rev. Hogstad went out as a member of that, but was supported by the conference.

THE HISTORY OF THE MISSION

Rev. J. P. Hogstad and wife arrived in Madagascar in the fall of 1887, and journeyed on to the interior where they remained for a year while studying the language. In the fall of 1888 they arrived at Ft. Dauphin. That was a long and very difficult journey, especially for Mrs. Hogstad; for the roads were poor and the journey was far from safe because of the fighting that was going on among the tribes and because of the robber bands. But they got through safely, and soon established themselves, gradually becoming accustomed to conditions in general. The fact that they understood the language was of great help to them, as they were able to converse with the natives. Rev. Hogstad was well fitted for the work, physically as well as spiritually. He was a large, well-built man, practical and able in

Missionary co-workers of the Halvorsons. Standing: Wm. Trygstad, Nellie Dahl, P. A. Bjelde, Sr. Caroline Thompson, Sr. Mette Hagen, and J. P. Hogstad. Seated: Mrs. Wm. Trygstad, Mrs. Bjelde, M. J. Stolee, Mrs. Stolee, and Mrs. Hogstad. J. P. Hogstad (upper right) founded the American Lutheran Mission in Ft. Dauphin.

many ways. He understood many kinds of work, learned the language quite easily, was gifted with a good temper, a cheerful disposition, and a strong faith, all gifts that are needed by missionaries who, like Rev. Hogstad, must break down all barriers, and take up the struggle against heathenism.

Arriving at Ft. Dauphin, tired after the lengthy journey, they had to crawl into a rickety Malagasy hut, and there they lived till Rev. Hogstad could build one that was somewhat larger (about two years). In the meantime the mission ship, *Paulus*, brought material from Norway for building a house, and, with that material, Rev. Hogstad soon managed to have a house built. That is our present mission station building.

At that time Ft. Dauphin did not have any regular connection with the outside world, and the Hogstads had to live on what the land produced. When, on rare occasions, the *Paulus* anchored in the bay, they enjoyed festive meals for a few days, and when the ship left they were supplied with some provisions. But, unfortunately, they were not in possession of refrigerators or cold storage places, and the provisions did not keep long in that climate. It must have been most difficult for Mrs. Hogstad to keep house in those days. Eggs, rice, meat, and different kinds of root vegetables were all that they were able to get in the line of provisions. Fortunately, she was a good housekeeper, and was well able to prepare tasty meals from what could be had, in different ways. More difficult it was to take care of the house. Ft. Dauphin was, at that time, mainly a pile of sand, and the strong east wind that continually whistled about our ears, swept sand into every nook and corner. Of course all missionaries are prepared to suffer lack of various kinds when they leave a civilized country and set out to take up work among uncivilized heathens. But there was a vast difference between what those who took the lead in the struggle against heathenism had to go through and the experiences of us who came later. We do well in remembering them lovingly and with deep respect.

When they arrived on the field, they were well received by members of the government, and they even found a congregation there; but, in order not to infringe on the work of others, Rev. Hogstad soon began to build a church. At the same time he began a school for children in the Independent Church of the London Missionary Society with Ra Benjamin as teacher. The same year he also began a school for teachers with ten pupils. A prominent officer by the name of Rainiketamanga assisted in the teaching. The following year several of those pupils were baptized, and sent out into the district as temporary teachers. In the spring of 1889, he sent two men into the interior to get some workers from there, and in the fall he succeeded in getting five helpers. One of them—Raveljaona—is still in the work. When those workers from the interior arrived the former pupils were called back to continue their studies, and they, together with several others, attended school for a year and a half. In 1891 all of them were sent out as workers at 14 different outstations.

Mrs. Hogstad also did her best to help in the work and, among other helpful doings, she gathered a group of girls whom she instructed in handwork, etc.

Ft. Dauphin was at that time a garrison city. Besides the governor and the civil officers, many military officers and soldiers were there. The leading officers were Christian Protestants. They were very much interested in missions and did their best to help Hogstad in the work. All the Christian officers were obliged to attend church regularly, and their children to attend school. The governor himself preached quite often and attended the services regularly. He called in the members of the Tanosy tribe and ordered them to send their children to day school. When Hogstad sent the above mentioned teachers out to work, they received copies of the following letter from the governor and special orders to carry the letters with them:

"Hereby it is declared that you, 'N.N.,' have been appointed by the government to teach in the city of 'N.N.' Therefore your work will be to instruct people so that they may learn to know the truth. You teach them to read and write so that they may develop in the right way and learn how to worship the true God as they should, in the district where you are stationed. For that reason you must not waste your time in doing anything but teaching. And if you do not do that which it is your duty to do, and either waste your time or do something that might be harmful to the government, then you will be doing what is wrong, and shall be punished for it.

Ft. Dauphin, August 29, 1891,
Andriamarovon[y], 12th Degree of Honor
Governor"

An officer was sent with each teacher that he might install him in his new position. Each year the pupils were called in to take examinations, and the governor gave prizes to the most diligent among them. Because the Tanosy people both feared and hated the government, and looked distrustfully upon Missionary Hogstad and the "new doctrine," they were ordered to assemble in court at Ft. Dauphin. That took place in 1891. There the governor delivered a lengthy message, attempting to make clear to them that, when both the government and the missionaries were so anxious to have their children get an education, it was for the best of them all. Finally he distributed gifts among the parents. It was the formerly mentioned Andriamarovony who was governor at the time, and he seemed to have taken Christianity very seriously.

Rev. Hogstad was wise enough to unite his work with that which had already been begun by the independent people, from the very beginning, without "stepping on their toes." Thus, little by little, he gained such influence over them that they willingly placed the entire leadership in his hands. And those who know the Hovas, especially the independent people, will understand that, in order to get that position, Hogstad must have been quite a church diplomat. Through consultation with the London Missionary Society in Tananarive, the Norwegian Mission Society got the work at Ft. Dauphin turned over to them, and in 1892 Rev. Shaw came down and turned over the Independent Congregation and their church to Hogstad.

Though Hogstad led the work personally, he understood clearly, from the very beginning, that the most important factor in the work of spreading the Gospel and the furthering of the Kingdom of God among the heathens does not belong to the missionary alone, but to native workers. He immediately began a school where native workers might be trained, and was happy to find among them some gifted people who had already had more or less instruction through the independent workers. But they were few in number, and for that reason he was not able to spread the work as he had hoped to do. Before workers can be had, they must become Christians, and that takes time, especially at the founding of a mission; for the missionaries must first learn the language and become acquainted with the people, and, little by little, learn to understand

A Christian marriage ceremony in Ft. Dauphin.

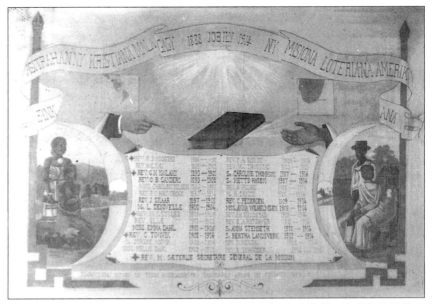

Poster commemorating the 25th anniversary of American Lutheran missionaries in Ft. Dauphin (1888-1914). Rev. M. Saeterlie is listed as the general secretary of the mission. P. J. Hogstad, Gabriel Isolany, P. C. Halvorson, Caroline Nilsen, and Eugene Rateaver are also listed.

conditions in general. Many of those with whom they have worked, of whom much is expected, slide back into their former mode of life, and cannot be used as teachers or evangelists.

When beginning a work, it is of vast importance to lay a good foundation, and not least in mission work. Everyone will understand that, when beginning a mission, it is of vast importance, not only to lay a good foundation but to get good material with which to build, to learn to know the people, understand the condition they are in, in order to lead in the right direction from the very beginning. When the work is planned and organized, it is difficult to change it and work on in another direction. That it is very difficult for missionaries who are perfect strangers on their arrival to find the right way of beginning work in a land where there is neither history or traditions to help in laying plans is easily understood. And even if they do know something about the early history and the character of the people, it is not the gift of many to "live as a barbarian for the sake of the barbarians, or as a Greek for the sake of the Greeks," in such a way that one might understand how to organize them in a way that is most fitting for their needs. But Hogstad seems to have understood how to go about that, and we owe him much gratitude for his clear understanding of the problems that lay before him and for the energetic work that he understood in order to solve the problems. It is not our intention here to say that his organization of the work was so entirely perfect that no flaw was cleaving to it. There were deficiencies—difficult problems, to be sure. We felt, for instance, that the school work had a more prominent place than direct evangelical work, and that nominal Christians, especially officers, had joined the church. That was detrimental to the congregation, and—at least at that time—would prevent the Gospel from spreading among the Tanosy. And, finally, the work towards self-support was not stressed enough. But our idea is that the mission work on the field was so widely spread that there is ample room for the congregation to grow and develop in different ways throughout the district, and that the principles for growth and self-support in the heart of true Christians must grow and flourish.

CHAPTER 7
A QUEEN GAVE HER BLESSING:
100 YEARS AGO IN MADAGASCAR

BY CONRAD HALVORSON

WHEN MY GRANDFATHER LANDED IN THE STEAMING PORT OF TAMATAVE, MADAGASCAR, A CENTURY AGO, HE WAS DRESSED IN THE HOMESPUN (WOOLEN) CLOTHING COMMON TO HIS HOMELAND OF NORWAY.[51] To the suggestion of an English missionary that he change into cooler clothing, the Rev. Nils Nilsen answered, "What was good enough for Norway is certainly good enough for Madagascar."

The Conrad Halvorson family in Madagascar, 1935.

Pastor Nilsen had set out for Madagascar in 1866 with the Rev. John Engh in a sailing vessel owned by the Norwegian Mission

---

51. This essay was published in *The Lutheran Standard* in September 1967. Pastor Conrad Halvorson was born in Ft. Dauphin to Peter and Antonette Halvorson, and served as a missionary in the Ft. Dauphin area for 27 years. When this article was published, Conrad was a Lutheran pastor in Rice Lake, Wisconsin.

Society. They intended to begin Lutheran mission work on the island.

Two men, alone in a country whose language and customs were entirely unknown to them, did not seem to offer a very promising prospect for mission work. But this year the centennial of Lutheran missions is being celebrated in the island nation by the 243,453-member Malagasy Lutheran Church, which has 150 pastors and 1,700 lay workers serving in more than 2,000 congregations.

The two missionaries were introduced to some of the uncertainties of their new life—including robbers—as they proceeded from the port to the capital of Tananarive. Today this trip takes one short day by train; it took them almost two weeks by palanquin (carrying chair). There they devoted a year to language study.

For a year the pioneer missionaries were alone, although some English missionaries were of great help to them. At the conclusion of their year of language study, their two fiancées arrived from Norway. The young couples were married in Tananarive by Bishop Hans Schreuder, pioneer missionary to Zululand, Africa, who had accompanied the young women on the ship. Mrs. Nilsen not only brought along her household linens (since no cloth was available locally) but also brought a spinning wheel which became invaluable in the years to follow.

Before leaving the island, Bishop Schreuder took time to examine possible mission sites. It was decided that the two young couples should begin work among the Betsileo people, a thrifty, energetic, and populous group located in the central highlands.

After a tiresome and dangerous four-day trip, again by palanquin, the Nilsens and Enghs arrived at the large town of Betafo (which means "many roofs"). They were the first white people to come to this area. So curious were the Malagasy to see white people that they came by droves to look at them. The missionaries lived in a rented one-room native hut, with one door and one window. Often these openings were filled with brown heads peeking in at the strange white men. At meal time they would disappear—it is not polite for a Malagasy to stare at people during meals.

Madagascar was ruled by a queen in those days.[52] When she

52. Ranavalona II.

heard that the missionaries had gone to the Betsileo people, she feared for their safety and sent soldiers to inform her subjects that these white people had her blessing. Furthermore, she asked them to permit the missionaries to teach and preach in their midst.

So the Lutheran mission in Madagascar was founded on December 5, 1867. Less than two years later, on April 11, 1869, two men of noble birth were baptized—first members of the Malagasy Lutheran Church.

The first Lutheran church was built at Betafo, and Pastor Engh continued working there for many years. The Nilsens left after some months to begin work in a neighboring community called Masinandraina. Later they moved to Loharano, where they remained until their departure for a furlough after nearly 20 years of service. Three much-loved hymns in the present Malagasy Lutheran Hymnal were written by Pastor Nilsen.

A forerunner of The American Lutheran Church began mission work in the far south of Madagascar in 1888. From the beginning Lutherans have worked in harmony. We share the same seminary, printing house, and hymnal. You can worship in any Lutheran church in the nation and expect to find the same service. The Malagasy Lutheran Church was formed in 1950, combining the work of the Norwegian Mission Society, the former Lutheran Free Church, and the former Evangelical Lutheran Church. The constitutional convention was held in 1952.

A major effort in the mission program has been to establish an indigenous church—supported by the people themselves and not by the church in the homeland. This idea has caught on. For some time the Betsileo Christians have supported their own work. The president of the Lutheran Church in Madagascar is a Malagasy, and the regional and general synods are controlled by the Malagasy people.

A hundred years ago all the people of the region were heathen, caught in the darkness of paganism and its indescribable forms of sin. Now the church is no longer foreign, but has become an accepted part of the life of the Malagasy people. From the cathedral-like church in Betafo one can see several red brick churches dotting the pleasant green valley below, a silent testimony to the power of God's Word. "It is the Lord's doing and it is marvelous in our eyes."

CHAPTER 8
THE LEGACY OF NILSEN AND HALVORSON MISSIONS IN MADAGASCAR

BY JAMES AND SONJA HALVORSON

THE CHILDREN, GRANDCHILDREN, AND GREAT-GRANDCHILDREN OF PETER AND ANTONETTE HALVORSON GREW UP LEARNING MUCH ABOUT THEIR INTERESTING RELATIVES WHO SPENT SO MUCH TIME AND ENERGY WORKING IN AND TALKING ABOUT MADAGASCAR, A FASCINATING ISLAND OFF THE SOUTHEAST COAST OF AFRICA THAT IS ROUGHLY THE SIZE OF OREGON AND CALIFORNIA COMBINED. I was one of the grandchildren who enjoyed time with Antonette Halvorson (1870-1966), and for me this experience was primarily an immersion in storytelling—I learned about the mission work in Madagascar, about the difficulties people encountered living there, and about the first fruits of the Gospel as it worked among the people.

Antonette, Olaf, Ruth, and Conrad (on stilts) near Ft. Dauphin, c.1913.

127

Many of these tales are collected in the missionary memoir entitled *Loharano (The Water Spring)*. In addition to her storytelling, Grandma painted old photographs with watercolors to preserve the feel of Madagascar as she remembered it, she wrote numerous letters about the country, and she encouraged others to complete missionary work there as they were able. Sonja and I have written this story as a tribute to the Nilsen-Halvorson missionaries and their influence on our lives.

Most of grandmother's adult stories focused on the work of her husband, P. C. (Peter) Halvorson, or "Papa Halvor," as his students called him. Grandmother described Papa Halvor with such respect and awe. And she highlighted the stories she told with old pictures showing Malagasy warriors and their spears and leather shields, fascinating witch doctors, fearsome crocodiles, and of course festive church gatherings involving lots of fellow missionaries, church leaders, and Malagasy Christians. Grandmother also told us how she taught sewing and the Bible in her Ft. Dauphin home, the unusual look of the flora and fauna in Madagascar, and countless other memories. The relating of their adventures sounded so much like Huck Finn to us, mixed with the religious aspect of training numerous leaders for church and government work.

As time wore on, we grandchildren and cousins also gathered to see and hear about Madagascar from Uncle Conrad (Peter and Antonette's son) and Aunt Gladys. We saw the beautiful flowers and animals of this land beyond the seas—a place beyond our comprehension of location—something like *Gulliver's Travels* or another far-out adventure. Conrad always expressed the beauty of the people and the land, and the exciting adventure of a life focused on training future leaders for Madagascar and the Church. These memories remained with us strongly, even after Conrad and the rest of the Halvorson-Nilsen clan had returned from the Madagascar mission field in the late 1950s. Eventually, a simple thought percolated to the surface—could Sonja and I one day visit Madagascar ourselves, and see this beautiful land and people in person?

Visiting Madagascar: A Dream Realized

In the 1980s, our idea about visiting the Halvorson-Nilsen mission roots in Madagascar came alive when we met a Malagasy man named Solo at our church in St. Paul, Minnesota. We had become acquainted with Solo recently through a shopping trip in which we helped him purchase clothing in preparation for a typical Minnesota winter—an odd experience for Solo, since he was from a tropical climate, the current temperature in Minnesota was nearing 90 degrees, and we were planning to buy clothes for a possible chill of 20 degrees below zero. After this shopping trip, we also had the privilege of having Solo with us for Christmas in Sinai, South Dakota, where he met James' father, Paul Halvorson, the eldest son of Peter and Antonette, a man born in Madagascar himself. Solo returned to Madagascar, but in 1993 he returned our hospitality by hosting our son Pete, as he completed his medical school training. You can read more about Pete in Chapter 9 of this book.

Solo taught us much about Madagascar, and after this initial experience we had a second opportunity to host a Malagasy man named Dr. Doxie. Dr. Doxie stayed with us for two years while he attended Bible school at our church in St. Paul. From him we heard many stories about Madagascar as it is today, and we began reading mission and travel books about the island country. Another new Malagasy friend, Dr. Daniel, who was also visiting the Twin Cities, supplied us with additional information. (Dr. Daniel was born in Betafo, Madagascar, where Great-Grandfather Nilsen and Pastor Engh started the first Lutheran church.)

We were now getting excited about an actual trip to Madagascar, in which we could visit sites related to the historic Halvorson-Nilsen missions, and learn about the current state of the Malagasy Lutheran Church. We continued our preparation by sending electronic mail to Malagasy and American friends living in Madagascar. Finally, we asked for advice from our missionary friends, Pastor Oliver and Gene Carlson, who were going to be in Madagascar in the autumn of 2000—precisely the time that we were thinking of going. Slowly but surely, our dream of visiting this beautiful island nation was becoming a reality! But what would happen when we actually arrived? Would there be any material or spiritual remains left of the Halvorson and Nilsen missions that began so long ago?

Sonja and I finally began our trip to Madagascar in September 2000, and we remained there through much of October 2000. Our trip took place during the dry season—a good time of the year to visit tropical Madagascar. The plane ride itself was an adventure—it took over 30 hours, and involved Boeing 777, 747, and 737 aircraft and a 340 Eurobus jet. The flights were long, but we were well fed. God constantly provided for us. We were met at the airport by Dr. Doxie's aunt and uncle, and this gave us another opportunity to reacquaint ourselves with a family that we had met earlier in St. Paul. Doxies' aunt and uncle took us around Tananararivo, the capital city, and hosted us in their home for several days. In the evenings while we were there—right in their home—we listened to beautiful music played by a professional musician. They took us to the King's House, where we saw a fancy chair, or palanquin, like the kings or important missionaries rode over a century ago. During these days, we also met Americans working with the Lutheran church, visited a Lutheran hospital, and saw in general how Christians are serving the people of Madagascar.

We have the following general observations about Madagascar. The people that we met were beautiful and quick to return a smile. We quickly learned that on average their everyday life is much harder than ours in America. Poor road conditions cause difficult driving, and pedestrians seemed constantly in danger on the roads, where cars have the right-of-way. The people in Tananarive were usually up early and seemed very active. Street venders quickly had charcoal heating pots ready to serve customers whenever we were out, although we usually ate in private homes or restaurants. Banks and other businesses were typically closed for two hours at noon, and then for the day by 4:00 p.m.

Our breakfasts were usually coffee or tea, French bread with jam, cheese, and eggs. Evening meals were served after 7:00 p.m.

These were very tasty and varied considerably, but rice was a common theme. Although we were seldom out after dark, we felt very safe and never had anything stolen. Hotels in Madagascar were quite inexpensive ($8 to $15 in 2000), except at special tourist or business hotels, which could be priced at $60 or higher. Meals usually cost between $2 and $5, and they were somewhat formal—meaning we had nice table cloths, napkins, and silverware, plus attentive service. Half our stay was in Malagasy or missionary homes, where we were given the best room, treated as royalty, fed very well, protected, loved, and spoken to in English.

THE VISIT TO ANTSIRABE

Our plan of action in Madagascar was to visit significant Norwegian and American Lutheran mission sites, and to focus in particular on Antsirabe, Betafo, Loharano, and Ft. Dauphin—places where we knew our relatives had lived and worked in the late 19th and early 20th centuries. Along the way we would greet our new Malagasy friends and welcome their help, as time and schedules permitted. We were searching for the mission sites associated with Peter and Antonette Halvorson, who were missionaries from 1897-1916, but also for any earlier sites that might be associated with the original work accomplished by our great-grandparents Nils and Inger Nilsen (missionaries from 1867 to 1886). In addition, we hoped to see what we could of Conrad and Gladys Halvorson's work after 1932, including places where their children and our cousins might have lived (Solveig, Glenn, and Phillip). We were really quite uncertain about all of this—it was very possible that we would find nothing at all, or that we would find a few of the actual buildings and landscapes that we had imagined so vividly in our childhood. Only time and God's grace would tell!

Our first stop was the inland city of Antsirabe, which our guidebook said was established by the Norwegian Lutheran missionaries Borgen and Rosaas in 1872.

Loharano (The Water Spring) describes the activities of a Mr. Borgen who worked with the Nilsens in the late 1860s, and we wondered with some excitement if this was the same man. Antsirabe is a beautiful city about 1,500 meters above sea level, with a current population of about 100,000. It has thermal baths, wide streets, and a number of European-based businesses producing products such as Loharano-brand water, dairy products, wine, and beer. It is also the headquarters of the Norwegian Mission Society, the organization (based in Stavanger) that originally started mission work in Madagascar back in 1867. The city of Antsirabe also reflects the heritage and traditions of Chinese workers who, under French rule, built several railroads to the capital of Tana and other places. The original train tracks were narrow gauge, and they are now used mostly for cargo and a few limited passenger services. Chinese-style rickshaws called "pousse-pousse" are still in evidence, however, and everywhere we saw the drivers (or runners), who were quite persistent but friendly.

The trip to Antsirabe from Tana was 169 kilometers, which we completed entirely by car. Along the way, we had a tire blowout in a small town. (This is a common experience in Madagascar.) Our Malagasy friend Solo, his wife, Lalao, and Laloa's brother (the driver) took us to Antsirabe and served as our guides. The morning after our arrival, we visited the Norwegian Mission Society compound and the Missionary Kids' School, and we even met the Norwegian director of these programs. We inquired about Loharano and other historic Nilsen mission sites, and received some basic directions and contacts in those areas. Then we went to visit Solo's friends at a local government hospital, who also knew the Lutheran hospital director.

The Lutheran hospital in Antsirabe had just celebrated its 100th birthday, and we were introduced to the staff as Nils Nilsen's great-grandchildren. We were met by the administrator, and a little later by four surgeons, who showed us their facilities and patients. The waiting room was large, and the administrator said that this room was also the chapel, where devotions were shared with the group at the beginning of each day. We felt like fancy inspectors general, and Sonja said, "Do you realize the honor we are being shown? Let's not take too much of their time." We chose to leave after a short but fascinating visit, and noted on our way out the new monument that indicated the hospital's 100th anniversary.

Later, we attended services at a large Lutheran church in Antsirabe that must have held 1,000 people. We sat near the front with Norwegians and our Malagasy friends, and later we had the opportunity to talk with a Norwegian missionary mother. I stated that many from both Norway and the United States are very critical of missionaries because they change the cultures of people. This young mother quickly responded in perfect English: "If one does not believe that Jesus is the only way, there is no reason to go, to tell about his love and forgiveness." Through conversations like these, we began to consider more deeply the challenges that missionaries and relief workers face in the field, and the importance of balancing missionary work with respect for imbedded cultural values and beliefs.

In all, the worship service lasted three hours and included the participation of five wonderful choirs. It all clearly expressed this community's gratitude to God for His love and forgiveness, and we were deeply moved.

Finally, we found the Antsirabe School for the Blind and made an appointment to return to visit the new director. The Lutheran School for the Blind was started at the Loharano congregation some 75 years ago. At that time, a missionary observed local people with blindness and the struggles they endured, and he found a way to bring them together at Loharano. A few years later, a Norwegian woman arrived, saw the pressing needs of the group, and returned to Norway to obtain special schooling and a certificate to teach the blind. She served as the school's first director. Eventually, the school moved from Loharano to a special campus in Antsirabe, where it is today. The buildings are distinguished by their Norwegian design, attractive roofs, and solar panels. During our stay, we met the second director of the school, a Malagasy woman, who was now retiring. We also had a chance to speak with the new (third) director, a Malagasy man.

The Engh and Nilsen Mission in Betafo

That Saturday we headed out toward Betafo, the place where it all started for the Nilsens in Madagascar. After a year of language training near the capital, Rev. Nils Nilsen and Rev. John Engh moved to Betafo in 1867 to begin their missionary work among the people. These men and their new wives were the first Lutheran missionaries in Madagascar. Would there be any traces left of their work?

As usual, we remembered Jesus' words, and asked for his guidance to secure an appointment with the people we should meet at the next stop. The ride to Betafo was on a good bituminous pavement with rich, small farmlands of wheat and other grains nearing harvest. The area was dry, and the rice planting was just beginning. Along the way, we tried to locate the village named Masinandraina that Grandma Antonette had described in *Loharano (The Water Spring)*, but at this point we could not find it. At last, we approached the village of Betafo.

Near the town and off the main highway, we passed a church or two that looked like they could be old mission sites, but then across a lake we saw something that looked more stately and promising. We headed up the road to the church, and there we saw a sign reading "Engh Boulevard." We had arrived, for John Engh was the missionary partner of Nils Nilsen way back in 1867—a man who had worked 20 years in Madagascar and returned with the Nilsen family. We walked around the churchyard and found a parsonage; there we met a regional pastor who amazingly knew of both Engh and Nilsen.

The pastor showed us a house that could have been built in the mid 1860s and used by Norwegian families, that is, the missionaries we were trying to locate. The structure was not used now because the roof needed fixing. As we walked to the church, we saw several youth playing Foosball (the table game) and other diversions on the beautiful Saturday afternoon. The women were getting ready for the Sunday celebration and the dinner afterwards. They had cut up meat and prepared other food for the next day. We heard that the church building had room for 400 worshipers, but close to 500 people actually attended each Sunday. (Later, the pastor asked if we could help with the expenses of putting in a larger balcony to serve the many attendees—Americans are often asked to support the rebuilding of churches when they visit.) Near the church was a brightly painted ox cart that they used to take donations of food and handicrafts to the market and sell for other church needs.

We went into the wooden church building, and there on the wall was a picture of the bearded Pastor John Engh. The regional pastor said that a few of Engh's relatives had been to this building, but that we were the first relatives of Nils Nilsen to visit that he knew of. Then came the youth for their choir and dance practice for the Sunday service. We had the privilege of seeing and hearing these children of God sing about Jesus. Their harmony and clearness was awesome. The choir leader, who was also an English teacher in the school, asked us to sing for them, and so we sang a praise song in English. This was "another goodie from God," as Aunt Alida Halvorson Brecke used to say.

We said good-bye to the regional pastor, the local pastor, and the choir director, and then headed toward our car. As we looked down at the lake, we were reminded of the setting in which Jesus preached the Sermon on the Mount so long ago. What an awesome site this was, as the early evening shadows crept up from the natural amphitheater below, and the lake reflected the fading sun and the village of Betafo in the distance. Engh and Nilsen had selected an awesome site for the first Lutheran church in Madagascar that would tell of the love and forgiveness of Jesus.

SEARCHING FOR GRANDMOTHER'S BIRTHPLACE

Just before we left Minnesota for Madagascar, I reviewed grandmother's *Loharano* book and wrote down some of the key places she had lived and visited. Grandmother mentioned that she was born in Masinandraina. To assist us in locating older villages like this, we brought along a Norwegian map of Madagascar from 1892 that our cousin Coral had given us. This map showed smaller villages like Masinandraina, but the recent maps of Madagascar that we had did not. Our host, Solo, and his brother-in-law the taxi driver did not know this town either, but they asked a lot of questions and eventually had an idea of its general location. However, they were told not to look for road signs (since there weren't any) but rather for key physical features on the road. With that, we were on our way.

We left Betafo and traveled east toward Antsirabe, with the goal of finding Masinandraina somewhere in between the two towns. The sun was setting, and we turned off the highway onto a dirt road that seemed to have the right physical markings. We hoped it would take us to the second Lutheran church that Nilsen started, and the place that grandmother and her sister were born. A wooden bridge was in front of us, and at the moment, it was full of cows. We waited for the cows to cross, and then Sonja and I got out to inspect the bridge. It looked OK, so our driver slowly crossed the structure by following two tire paths that just fit our wheels. The banks were near our doors, and the sharp hills almost caused the car to rub the ground. A bike and a cow were ahead of us so we waited again until we could get up enough speed to make the next hill without harming anyone.

For the next 20 minutes, we traveled along this dirt road as it wound its way up to a high ridge. Here we found a Catholic church and a school—signs of productive missionary activity—but we continued on in hopes of finding the Lutheran church built by Nilsen. Soon we located a second compound with a Lutheran church and school. We stopped at the house next door and asked about the origins of the buildings. The pastor was gone, but his wife greeted us cheerfully and showed us around as if she had been waiting for us. She was not in a hurry, nor harried with things that needed to be done. Finally, she pointed toward a depression and said that Nilsen's church had been there. She said that she didn't believe Nilsen had lived in Masinandraina but that he had started this church from Betafo and lived in Betafo. This woman was the French teacher at the Lutheran school and spoke enough English to communicate with us.

Next, the pastor's wife took us into the Lutheran church, where we saw a picture of another missionary on the wall and a typical Norwegian altar setting like the one in my birth church in Sinai, South Dakota. We sang a few hymns together and prayed in our respective languages, and we felt a bond with our distant family members who had planted these seeds of faith and had raised up the name of Jesus. Then we visited the graves of Norwegians who had died early deaths and others who had died in middle age or old age. This churchyard was holy ground. We learned that the Norwegians had sent many missionaries to continue the work of the pioneers, and that some had died very young. There was much evidence of faithfulness along with hardships. We left in the dark with a deep sense of peace, knowing that we had visited Nilsen's missionary roots and the place that Grandmother Antonette had described as her birthplace in *Loharano*. Yes, another "goodie from God."

THE VISIT TO LOHARANO

Grandmother Antonette named her book *Loharano (The Water Spring)* because her family had spent considerable time doing missionary work in an inland village or district named Loharano, which was also the source of numerous natural water springs. We had asked about this area at the Norwegian Mission Society headquarters in Antsirabe, and by using information from local drivers and our 1892 map, we were able to find the village east of Antsirabe some 40 miles. Along the way to Loharano, we passed small towns and crossed several bridges spanning dry streams. We even met a man who turned his car completely around when he learned where we were going. He then proceeded to drive straight to the village, with us following. Little did we know that we were about to make contact with one of the most tangible links to our family's missionary past in Madagascar.

We began our visit to Loharano at the Lutheran High School for the Blind. It was now late afternoon, and we met the school director, his wife, and their baby. The house was a two-story home of Norwegian design, built in the early 1900s and consisting of offices, dorms, classrooms, and a dining room. The small square contained flowers, a cow, a driveway, and a few play areas. Off to the side was a cemetery with many Norwegian names. The director had heard about Nils Nilsen, and pointed out a well house that covered a spring that Nilsen had discovered in the 1870s or 1880s. This was the spring that the Nilsen family had drunk from until they left for America in 1886. The director said there were four such springs within view of this place.

A 90-year-old pastor in Loharano recalls his father's work with Nils Nilsen.

At this point, a truly amazing thing happened. The director's wife went to see a retired Malagasy pastor in the area who soon arrived at the school. The pastor's name was Razafinjoelina Andrias, and he had just turned 90 in October 2000. After a few moments, we learned that this man's father had served with Nils Nilsen as a catechist at the Loharano Mission Station, and that Razafinjoelina had continued this work in the area churches. After a few brief introductions, we asked the pastor questions, and our friend Solo interpreted the answers for us. But this process soon became too exhausting, so we just asked the pastor to talk while we recorded the interview on a camcorder. (Solo also took notes.) The pastor referred to a history book about Madagascar with dates and more information. When the interview was over, we were introduced again, and the pastor became fully aware that James was the great-grandson of Nils Nilsen. The pastor came over to hug James with tears in his eyes. Then the director of the school said, "Madagascar will never forget Nils Nilsen." We concluded this exchange by asking Pastor Andrias why his eyes were so good that he could read without glasses. He responded with a smile, "The good Malagasy food."

Here is a summary translation of what Pastor Razafinjoelina Andrias, born October 12, 1910, told us about the early missionary work of Nils Nilsen in the Loharano area. (The text was translated by Solo and recorded in English by Sonja.)

"At first, people in the region didn't like the Bible, but one Malagasy agreed to work with the Pastor. He decided to bring the Bible with him. At that time, it was dangerous to carry a Bible, so he put it into a small bag and covered the Bible with something and his glasses. He was intercepted by the enemy who came to see what he brought. The enemy tried to find something but saw only the glasses.

"In Ambanarive in 1867, the first church was built. A man named Ramakari was a Christian [there]. A friend asked for some Bibles for Ramakari, and the first Bible arrived in Loharano, but they were very fearful. He had to read it in the night and show it in the night. This was because they thought it would cause harm to them. So he read to them at night, and they prayed like this, "[May] Christianity be developed in this region." In 1872, Nils Nilsen arrived as an answer to their prayers. The first church was built in Loharano [with help] from Ambanarive. Each time the worship service [in Loharano] was finished, the Christians offered a final greeting for safety 'for [us] not to be killed in this church.' Every time they finished with worship, Pastor Nilsen said something that included the word *Bermanzo*, which means "more pains" [in Malagasy]. The Christians had many enemies and endured much pain. So Nils Nilsen was called *Bermanzo*.

"At first, Nilsen couldn't find someone from the region to help take care of his children, because the people in that region were fearful. They thought that if they helped Nilsen, some of their [own] children would become *Vaza* ('foreigners')." Finally, one woman accepted the job of taking care of Nilsen's children, but it was very difficult [for her] to make that decision. Nilsen was feared [by all], and life was very, very difficult for him and his family.

"One time Nilsen killed a *Zebu* ('cow'), and gave the meat to the people, but the people wouldn't take and eat. They threw it in the river, for they thought the *Zebu* was poisoned. Poisoning was practiced by many [at that time]. Even the queen was fearful of being poisoned, so she had many mirrors in her dining area. When she entertained guests, she could detect if someone added poison to her food. Nilsen's life was very difficult.

"Pastor Nilsen built a church even though the situation was bad. Some *Zirika* ('strong warriors') set a fire to some churches built in this region and burned them down, but [over time] the Christians rebuilt.

"The first Malagasy pastor at this [Lutheran] church in

Loharano was Reinitsimba from Antananarivo after 1872. Missionaries supervised by Nilsen liked this pastor. Reinitsimba was my father, and also the director of Bible study in Loharano for 27 years. He assisted Missionary Nilsen to accomplish this beginning Christian work. My father desired me to be at least a pastor, and so I became a pastor. I went to the [Lutheran] seminary in Fianarantsoa from 1933 to 1939, and was a student there where my father was also a teacher. I then worked in Betafo for 12 years."

Sonja and James Halvorson visit the Loharano church founded by Nils Nilsen. The original church was built in 1870.

After this amazing and emotional interview with Pastor Andrias, we walked to the Lutheran church past the school buildings. Pastor Andrias showed us a tree along the path where a three-month-old Nilsen boy [Herman] was buried. There was only an unmarked stone by the tree. Pastor Andrias said that the Nilsen's oldest boy (Gabriel) went back to Norway before the rest of the family [he later returned as a missionary]. The church also had a big sign indicating their 130-year anniversary (1870-2000).

The sun was now going down, so we said good-bye with many hugs, and left our brothers and sisters. The planted seeds had grown. The trip back was filled with wonderment at the privilege of meeting these key people without any previous contacts. This had been a heavenly hour in a heavenly atmosphere to hear of the struggles and victories in starting this congregation for Jesus by determined and faithful servants. Solo summed up all our feelings when he said "This story must be recorded."

EXPLORING FT. DAUPHIN

Ft. Dauphin (now called Taolagnaro) is a town of approximately 25,000 people on the southeast coast of Madagascar, where Peter and Antonette Halvorson began their mission work in 1897. Rev. J. P. Hogstad was a pioneer missionary in this area for the Conference of the Norwegian Lutheran Church of America, and Peter and Antonette Halvorson continued to support the Ft. Dauphin Mission Station by founding and constructing a boys' school, where future church and civic leaders might be developed. Antonette's brother, Gabriel Nilsen Isolany, along with his wife and Peter Halvorson's sister Inga, and Antonette's sister, Caroline Nilsen, also worked in this mission field, as did Conrad Halvorson and his family a generation later.

We remember family pictures of young Paul, Victor, and Frida in this setting, and later, young Conrad on stilts, and Ruth with her lemur, along with the photographs of the Halvorson and Nilsen families and other missionary workers. These early snapshots were often taken in front of Peter and Antonette's missionary home in Ft. Dauphin, which still exists, and now serves as the home of a Lutheran pastor and a catechist, as well as their families. Across the street from the old missionary home is a large stone Lutheran

Peter and Antonette's missionary home in Ft. Dauphin is still standing today (September 2002) and is used by Lutherans who serve the community.

church, where we enjoyed a worship service and an evening choir concert. The original, prefabricated wooden mission church that was sent piece by piece from Norway has been destroyed; this building was leveled by a storm when our missionary friend Steve Lellelid's father was schoolmaster and lived in the house Grandpa Halvorson built. It was a joy to visit this place with so many family memories. The Lutheran clinic, preschool and church are all on the same block. Grandpa's 105-year-old house and several similar houses are across the street. Banks, stores, post office, and government buildings are nearby.

The MK or "Missionary Kids" boarding house is a three-story building where the children of many Lutheran missionaries have

lived and attended school. Our cousins Solveig Halvorson Johanson, Glenn Halvorson, and Phillip Halvorson (the children of Conrad and Gladys) lived there. The boarding house is now called the Hotel Mahavoky, and it is owned by the mayor

The Hotel Mahavoky in Ft. Dauphin was once the location of the Missionary Kids' school.

of Ft. Dauphin. There is a grand entrance that leads into a hall. At the end of the hall stands a grand stairway to the dozen large hotel rooms. We had indoor plumbing (installed for the youth) with cold showers in a common location on the second floor. The cooking was done out back under a roof with open sides. We ate in style with good food and linen.

From the hotel, we looked south across a valley to the Lutheran cemetery, which included a missionary area. There were many names that reflect the American Lutheran effort of going and telling about Jesus. Many baby graves reflected the difficulties of childbirth and early childhood. It was there that we found the

Lutheran cemetery in Ft. Dauphin. The marker on the right is for missionary J. P. Hogstad.

gravestones of two Isolany babies (Gottfred and Clifford), two Halvorson graves (Anna and Herman), and the marker for Eugene Rateaver, a boy of mixed Malagasy and French parentage, whom Gabriel and Inga Isolany brought back to America for education at St. Olaf College. Roteaver later returned to Madagascar and worked for the Lutheran church in the Ft. Dauphin area. He was also imprisoned in the 1940s, when he and others supported the struggle for Malagasy independence from France. We heard that the Lutheran Mission Office in Chicago is looking for stories and contacts about these graves, and would like to restore the gravestones.

We spent the following days visiting Lutheran and Catholic churches in the area, worshiping with Malagasy Christians, and visiting medical sites and healing facilities. We arranged to have offering funds and gifts collected at the July 2000 Halvorson Reunion in South Dakota used to paint and repair Peter and Antonette Halvorson's Ft. Dauphin home. We also visited the missionary homes at the coastal retreat center in Libanona, where Peter and Antonette, Gladys and Conrad, and our cousins found relief from the very hottest weeks of the year. Many of these wooden houses, without electricity or telephones, are still owned by missionaries or relief organizations. The Indian Ocean is immediately to the south, with a beach to the west and a vista to the east. We swam at the beach and recalled stories of Grandpa P. C. and Conrad reading as they relaxed in the ocean water.

Climbing Mt. Pic St. Louis

Looking north from the second-floor veranda of the Mission-ary Kids' building (Hotel Mahavoky), we were able to view Mt. Pic St. Louis, with an elevation of 529 meters. This is the mountain that Peter Halvorson climbed in the year 1900 and then chiseled his name on a rock as a type of memorial. For years we had wanted to visit this place to see if his name was still there, and to carve our own names in the rock beside his. What better time to try this than the year 2000, exactly 100 years after Peter had made his historic climb? But now, we could also see that this mountain was probably a kind of lonely place to which grandfather could withdraw when he needed some alone time. It reminded us of the type of environment that Jesus searched out when he needed his own time for prayer and religious contemplation. The next day, Sonja and I decided to climb the mountain and have a look.

After making a few inquiries, we learned that Pic St. Louis took about two hours for strong hikers to climb, round trip. Our Hotel Mahavoky hostess, Elysee, offered to take a day off from her job and be our escort on this adventure. We left the next morning at 7:00 a.m., traveling by taxi to the base of the mountain. A seven-year-old boy skipped school and joined us. As we worked up the hill slowly but steadily, we were passed by hikers from other European coun-tries. We told them what we were looking for, and when they passed us again on the way down, they told us where to look for "the rock."

Due to a recent fire, there were very few trees left on the Pic St. Louis. Grass protected some of the slope that had once been the southern part of a rain forest, and an east wind brought moisture up the slope to supply much needed moisture and humidity. As we observed the slow deforestation of the mountain, we met men carrying huge bundles of sticks down Pic St. Louis to sell as fuel in the market. Soon we were above the tree line, and the wind blew our hats off. James suggested that Sonja just wait while the other three ascended to see the rock, but she insisted that the rest of us go ahead and that she would come at her own pace. The path was clearly made by hikers and not groomed by park employees. Except for some trees at the bottom and in a few creeks on the way up, we walked across little or no vegetation. The path had been worn by

A recent photo of P. C. Halvorson's name at the top of Mt. Pic St. Louis near Ft. Dauphin.

View of the Indian Ocean from Mt. Pic St. Louis.

hikers and had several large steps. Sonja was a trooper even to attempt this rough trail. Thank Jesus, we had only one fall. (I slipped and skinned my arm on the way down.)

This is not the first time that we would see environmental damage in Madagascar as a result of erosion or wood-gathering practices. Later in Madagascar we visited a private forest at Berenty. There we learned that there is no longer much wood for building basic wooden structures, and that when people harvest wood for cooking fuel, the trees are not replanted. Much of the southern part of Madagascar looks like Arizona now; it is very dry and rapidly filling up with sand dunes. This is in an area that once contained beautiful rain forests and several unique species of plants and animals. In the south, we also met a Japanese Ph.D. student who was doing research on the social life of lemurs, a primate unique to Madagascar. The Malagasy clearly have many challenges in the area of environmental protection and reforestation.

After four hours, we were on the top of Pic St. Louis and located "the rock," which was covered with hundreds of painted names. The wind was still strong, and we could hardly keep our hats on. We ate lunch on the leeward side of the rock and enjoyed the vista. We could see Ft. Dauphin to the south, and the hotel where we were staying. All of this was the mission field of Peter Halvorson and his associates. The Indian Ocean covered more than half of our vista, and other hills and mountains with few trees covered the rest. It was beautiful.

The rock itself stood 20 feet above the trail on top of the mountain. By going around to the back, we could climb on top, and near the northerly edge was the famous inscription that we were seeking: "P C Halvorson 1900." We also saw the more recent inscriptions "G. H." and "E. H." We assume these were from Erik's medical residency here with his mother and sister. At last, the goal of standing by the rock a century after Grandpa had visited his "lonely place" was accomplished.

Suddenly, a new realization came to us. Grandpa's decision to chisel his name and the date on that rock hadn't come from a simple trip up the Pic St. Louis in Ft. Dauphin, Madagascar. He had done this type of chiseling once before—with his twin brother Herman, on a farm in a faraway place, on the shores of Lake Sinai, South Dakota. The Christopher Halvorson family had recently constructed a sod house near Sinai—their home on the plains after leaving southeast Minnesota—and the teenage twins were herding cattle nearby, with a little time on their hands. They found a chisel and hammer and carved their names on a big rock by the lake—for all to see. Among other things, it probably meant "here we are, Lord—Peter and Herman, in our new home, in Dakota Territory." But now, in 1900, Peter's twin was far away in America, and he and his wife, Anna, would soon be raising and caring for Peter and Antonette's children—Paul, Victor, and Alida. In just a few years, Frida would be parted from her parents, too, living with Antonette's family back in Washington State. For these missionaries in a far-off and dangerous land, having a family often meant being separated from them. "How I miss my brother and his wife," Peter must have thought. "Lord, sometimes I wonder why I'm here, so far away from family. You called Antonette and me to this place, and we are here teaching, recruiting, and caring for these boys, so that one day they can be leaders in your church and this country's government. We need your refreshment and encouragement and direction for these days." Then, perhaps, after a long silence on this windy mountain, we imagine that he found a way to accept his life and praise his God: "Thank you, God, for the wisdom we need for this day and tomorrow. It is good to be here and to tell of your love and forgiveness. I am going down again now to be a part of the team of missionaries that you have sent to this beautiful island. Thank you for calling me and my partner, Antonette."

For some reason, literally walking in Peter Halvorson's steps up this mountain had helped us to understand him better, and to appreciate the many sacrifices that the Nilsens and Halvorsons had to make so long ago. With much to think about, we returned back down the mountain. The return trip took us over four hours, and by the time that we had returned, our taxi driver had given up on us and left. We began our walk back to town, and as the sun set, a second taxi drove by and offered us a ride the rest of the way. We returned to our hotel, had a shower, ate a wonderful meal, and went to bed. God had again protected us, and given us the experience of a lifetime.

We had further adventures in Madagascar, but our major goals of tracing the historic footsteps of the Nilsen and Halvorson missions had been accomplished. The seed planted by our grandparents and many others is producing more seed, and we have witnessed it. The congregations of the Malagasy Lutheran Church, as well as the churches of many other Christian denominations, are building a strong Christian base in this beautiful island nation. Social programs are on the rise in this country, and medical teams from Europe and America are bringing encouragement to the needy. And yet, some villages are still without schools, medical care, or Christian worship opportunities. There is still much to do in Madagascar.

On our trip, we met many educated young men and women— and older people too!—who have their hope in Jesus, and who are "working out their salvation" where they are—at school, at work, at church, at home, etc. Though the needs of the people are great, we received many smiles and greetings from friends and strangers alike. The Malagasy love to sing. What a joy to listen!

So thank you, friends—for helping us see what God has done and is doing in Madagascar. We are glad that Jesus sets our eyes on the future and beyond our daily life struggles. We all have HOPE.

CHAPTER 9
A GUIDE TO VISITING MADAGASCAR

BY PETER JAMES HALVORSON

 IN 1993, I WAS IN MY FOURTH YEAR OF MEDICAL SCHOOL, AND I WAS ABLE TO WORK OUT A TROPICAL ROTATION IN MADAGASCAR— AN EXOTIC LAND THAT MY PARENTS AND OTHERS IN THE FAMILY HAD ALWAYS TALKED ABOUT. My goal was to study tropical diseases and their treatment in a developing country. Fortunately, my family had recently made friends with a Malagasy gentleman named Solo, who had attended the University of Minnesota in the late 1980s. He and his family treated me royally while I was in the capital city of Antananarivo. But it was also helpful to have a strong family history in Madagascar. Because of Peter and Antonette Halvorson, I was able to enjoy the luxury of being much better connected than a regular tourist.

There are many exciting areas to explore in Madagascar. The capital city has a zoo and museum where you can see a wide variety of lemurs. There is a place where you can see original tribal dwellings and the homes of royalty, which spans two centuries. Antananarivo also offers what appears to be the world's largest open-air market. Wares from all over Madagascar and the world are being bartered off in this place. Further south in Ft. Dauphin, the home of Peter and Antonette Halvorson, there is a fantastic beach and the orphanage (now a hotel) that Peter and Antonette ran. There is also a nature preserve outside of Ft. Dauphin that allows you to experience lemurs and other Malagasy flora and fauna that are not found natively in other countries. Visiting Madagascar is truly amazing—just experiencing the people and the environment is exciting and eye-opening.

MEDICAL TRAINING IN MADAGASCAR

While doing my tropical medicine rotation in the jungles of eastern Madagascar, and in the arid areas in the southern part of the island, I encountered many tropical diseases. The list included malaria, filariasis (which includes elephantiasis), tuberculosis, intestinal worms (of the class Cestoda), and many other unusual protozoans and parasites. Fundamentally, Madagascar suffers from the same type of diseases that many other tropical nations do, and especially those in sub-Saharan Africa. Malaria is a significant problem, and it is a disease that is under-treated in Madagascar unless people become very sick. Although Malagasy people build up some resistance to malaria over time, it is still a leading cause of death in the country. In addition to this, Malagasy children routinely become dehydrated from parasites, viral diarrhea, or bacterial diarrhea. In the hospitals that I visited, patients with these ailments were the most common recipients of IV fluids for dehydration.

In general, I found that the Malagasy people were always very thankful for the help that we offered them. It is amazing to think of the conditions in the rooms at the hospital, and how different it is in American hospitals. In Madagascar, there were typically four patients to a room, and the patient's family would usually stay with the patient and attend to a lot of the nursing care and feeding. Family members would typically sleep on the floor or in the bed with the patient. And the patients had incredible pain tolerances. I remember one patient, a Malagasy man, who had an abscess in his chest. The abscess was slowly draining out his axilla (armpit). We operated on him to open up the abscess, and he was like a new man in 24 hours. He was so thankful.

We also encountered cancers, difficult deliveries, trauma, serious depression, and other psychological problems. In one of the places where I was stationed in eastern Madagascar, a village named Ankaramalza, a psychiatrist oversaw a work farm where people with

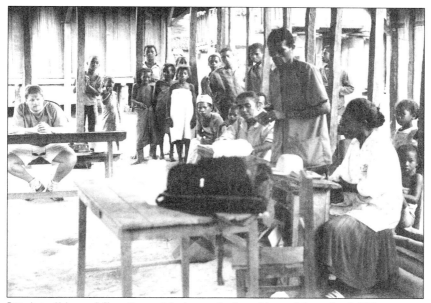

Peter James Halvorson (left) practices medicine in a remote village clinic near Ankovomalaza in 1993.

mental disorders from other villages could come and live. Interestingly, some of the best-looking crops and animals were located on this farm. In Ankaramalza, the patients were taken into the local people's huts to live, and they were considered part of the community. It took a while for me to fully understand this. Indeed, there were many days that a person would scream at me, and I was concerned that I had done something that was taboo in Malagasy culture. However, the staff informed me that the people were simply in the village for psychological and psychiatric treatment.

While I was in Ankaramalza, a woman was brought to us who had recently given birth in her village, and had continued to hemorrhage. She was brought to us by stretcher, with her newborn, at a distance of over 10 miles. With just IV fluids, we were able to take her from close to death to stable in just a few hours. If she had not reached us in time, she probably would have died.

The hospital in Ankaramalza had a small operating room with three surgical lights. The lights were powered by solar power, and we had a large operating room light (typical of what you might see in the United States) that would basically consume all the stored solar power in just one hour. So we usually used a 95-watt light bulb that would last long enough for an actual surgery to be completed. This brought home to me how very different Malagasy society is from what I was used to in America. Although I eventually worked in a more sophisticated Malagasy hospital (the Manaboro hospital outside Ft. Dauphin, which even featured an x-ray), the differences between our two medical systems was quite eye-opening. For another example, I had not done any dentistry work in my career until I arrived in Ankaramalza. However, tooth decay was rampant there, and soon I was learning how to use a hand drill and to mix up paste that I could use to fill a cavity. If they were available, dentists would certainly be very busy in any Malagasy village!

VISITING MADAGASCAR

Madagascar is an exciting place to visit, but before you go it's a good idea to consider your expectations and lay some basic groundwork. Work on patience, for the Malagasy do not generally move at the same speed as we do in the United States. This is vital to understand so that you can sit back and enjoy this beautiful country and its friendly people. Going from medical school in the States, where there is way too much to do in a short amount of time, to the relaxed pace of the tropics was a very difficult transition for me, but once I understood that I could not make it go any faster, I learned to enjoy the pace. Learning French, even just a little, was helpful. Along these lines, consider bringing a French/English dictionary.

Do not, and I repeat, do not try to see the whole country in a short period of time. If you leave the United States in the winter, remember that it is summer in Madagascar, and that it takes about two weeks to acclimate to the hot, humid weather. The capital city, Antananarivo, is relatively cool compared to the southern and eastern parts of the country that I visited. So the capital is a good place for transitioning. Give yourself some time to get used to the environment, and remember that you will probably get sick sometime during your stay in Madagascar. I was not feeling up to par about a third of the time due to viral gastroenteritis and malaria. However, when I was feeling well, I fell in love with this large island and the people on it.

The people of Madagascar are very friendly. Only in the capital city did I experience any problems with pickpockets. And the people who tried to rob me were only little kids, so I actually felt some remorse for stopping them. The rest of my time in Madagascar, I never had anything stolen. The people have warm smiles and harmonious voices. For sticking out in a crowd as a blond white man, I was always treated with respect. We could learn from this on how we treat others that are not the same ethnicity as we are—even if they are Swedish (he he). And get used to two-year-olds breast-feeding in public. It is very pure and natural. In fact, it is probably important for their nutrition as they are growing fast at that age. Why we are so worried about women breast-feeding in public here in America is beyond me.

Do not give out money. You can have a large crowd fighting over the money, and someone may get hurt. If while you are in Madagascar, you want to help the people in the area, give the money to the mission that you are staying at, or keep a list of worthwhile mission projects and send the money through official channels once you are back home. They can put that money to much better use toward helping the local people. Which reminds me it is helpful to contact a mission group such as SALFA or Global Health Ministries. They can get you set up with places to stay and chances to meet missionaries in the area.

Ft. Dauphin is where most of my Halvorson ancestry work was accomplished, as my parents have discussed in Chapter 8 of this book. Loharano is also an area of Nilsen/Halvorson influence. But since I was not there I will focus on Ft. Dauphin. The best way to get there is to fly from Antananarivo. The roads were not very good when I was there, but that was back in 1993. There is a cemetery at the southern end of town, overlooking the ocean, and it contains several graves of little Halvorsons that died at an early age. The cemetery was overgrown, and I would not have been able to find it if I had not met up with a missionary that had learned to swim from Conrad Halvorson. The other main attraction is the building next to the mission house. This is now a hotel and a restaurant. Order at the restaurant and then leave for an hour—your meal may be ready when you come back. This is the boys' home that Papa Halvorson built.

Of course, you must also go to the beach. There is a nice protected beach with perfect sand in the southwest corner of Ft. Dauphin. If you go straight south of town, you will run into the cemetery. When you are at the cemetery, look down toward the ocean. There is a road that goes west, and this is the one that you should take to the beach. As my parents describe in Chapter 8, people still seem to know about Papa Halvorson. Once again, dropping this name occasionally will be helpful for you. Northwest of Ft. Dauphin is the mountain on which Peter Halvorson wrote his name on a rock. It is quite a hike from the road. We were able to explain to a taxi driver that we were looking for the rock where the missionaries wrote their names. He was able to take us to a path, and after an hour hike—mostly uphill—we found the rock with P. C. Halvorson's writing and the date 1900. For a few more details about this interesting hike, read Chapter 8.

What to Bring

The following is a list of important items to bring if you visit Madagascar and Ft. Dauphin. You will need a small flashlight, sunscreen, mosquito repellent with 100 percent DEET, and mosquito netting that is big enough to be tucked under your mattress when you get into bed. (Most of these nets hang from hooks on the ceiling, and some hotels also provide them.) Have a water-purifying system (or tablets) and malaria pills. (I took one Lariam pill each week, starting a week before I left, but there are other options now.) For clothing, bring light clothes and shorts, light dresses for women, one pair of jeans, and dress-up clothes for church. It rains now and then, so bring an umbrella, sandals, tennis shoes, cameras and batteries, ziplock bags, no-wash hand soap (the antibacterial stuff), and—if you're venturing away from the nicer hotels—a light sleeping bag and a backpack to hold all this stuff. People with vision issues will need to bring plenty of contact solution and extra glasses.

Here are some optional items that I really found useful as an American male in my mid-20s: American toilet paper, ketchup, and a cookbook on how to make American food from scratch. (I found a recipe book at the Manaboro hospital guest house describing how to recreate American food in Madagascar using local ingredients—this was very helpful!) Along these lines, I suggest that you do not buy hamburger at the local markets, but purchase solid meat instead and find a way to grind it yourself.

If you want to give small gifts, you might want to bring the following items to the missionaries and local people: pens, Jell-O deserts and pudding mixes, toilet paper, balloons, stuffed animals, and movies. You might also consider bringing baseball hats. Everyone loves to have a baseball hat, and nobody cares what logo is on the cap—as long as it doesn't seem overtly capitalistic. They probably won't even mind if you offer them a Chicago Bears hat, but there may be limits here.

If you are interested in going to Madagascar, please feel free to contact me. I may even be able to help you get connected with a missionary group!

Peter James Halvorson
Edgerton, Wisconsin
December 2001

INDEX

Algiers, 42

alphabet, Malagasy, 19

American Lutheran Church, 60, 104, 125

Ancestor worship. *See* religion, traditional

Andriamarovony, Govenor, 118

Andrianamponinimerina, 9, 110

Andrias, Rev. Razafinjoelina, 138-40

Ankaramalza, 151

Antananarivo (Tananarive), 9, 18, 31, 40, 114, 124, 130

Antsirabe, 35, 38, 81, 131-33

Arnevaag, Norway, 56

Augsburg Publishing House, 4

Augsburg Seminary, Minneapolis, 60, 115

baobab tree (*Adansonia grandidieri*), 12, 47

baptism, 46, 49, 62, 117, 125

Bastille Day, 92

Battleground, Washington, 55-56, 90. *See also* Ridgefield, Washington

bee story, 3-4

Benjamin, Ra, 117

Bergen, Norway, 56

Betsileo, tribe, 9, 19; district of, 47, 125

Betafo, 11, 19, 21, 27, 124, 129, 134-36

Bezavona, Mt., 67, 82

Bible, translation, 9; studying, 46

Bjelde, P. A. and Mrs., 116

Borchgrevink, Dr. and Mrs., 43

Borgen, Mr., 43, 131

boys' school, Ft. Dauphin, 59-66, 74-75

Brecke, Alida. *See* Halvorson, Alida

cactus plant, 31, 65-66

candle making, 35

Cape of Good Hope, 8

Catholics, French, 9

cemetery, Ft. Dauphin, 92, 142-43, 153

Civil War, American, 8

coffee, 71

colonization, French, 8, 80-86, 111-13

Communion, sacrament of, 62

Conference of the Norwegian Lutheran Church of America, 60, 115

confirmation (rite), 62

Conrad, Joseph, 8

coronation, Ranavalona III, 9, 40-42

crocodile, 18, 37, 128

Dahl, Emma, 84

Dahl, Nellie, 116

Dahle, Rev. Lars, 19, 40, 43

Diego Dias, 8

disease, tropical, 150

Durban, 97-98

Eldorado, 55

elephant bird (*Aepyornis maximus*), 13, 37

elephant, 107

Elieser, 18, 22, 38, 49

Engh, Rev. John, early work, 21, 43, 135; first missionary to Madagascar, 10, 18, 123-24, 129; furlough, 49-50

England, passage to, 55-56, 97-98

erosion (soil), 145

ethnic sensitivity, 7

eucalyptus trees, planting, 46

Evangelical Lutheran Church, 4, 125

Evangelical Lutheran Church in America, 104

evangelism, Lutheran, 46

evangelist school (Ft. Dauphin), 72, 91-96

Fianarantsoa (seminary), 49, 69, 81, 91

fishing, 66-67, 71

Foreid, Maria, 40

Franzen, Miss, 42

Froid, Lillian Isolany, 100

Ft. Dauphin (Taolagnaro), 3, 59-86, 103-4, 118, 127, 141-47, 149, 152-54

Gibraltar, 91
God, Malagasy words for, 108

Hagen, Mette, 116
Halvorson, Alida, 5, 87-88, 99-100, 135, 146
Halvorson, Anna Boyd, 87, 100, 146
Halvorson, Anna Olivia, 99, 143
Halvorson, Antonette, birth, 21, 135; called as missionary to Madagascar, 59; childhood in Madagascar, 17, 22-49; children of, 66-67, 83, 87-90, 95, 99-100; ethnic sensitivity of, 7; Foreword, 1-2; furlough to South Dakota, 87-91, 100; legacy of, 5, 127-48; marriage, 57; memories of ocean travel, 49-55; move to Ridgefield, Washington, 57; visit to Norway, 56; work at Ft. Dauphin boys' school, 59-66
Halvorson, Arthur, 100
Halvorson, Christopher, 62, 146
Halvorson, Clifford, 100
Halvorson, Conrad, 5, 11, 67, 83, 87-89, 98-100, 123-25, 127-28, 131, 141-42, 153
Halvorson, David, 14
Halvorson, Felix, 4, 14
Halvorson, Frida, 5, 67, 83, 87-88, 90, 99-100, 141, 146
Halvorson, Gladys, 123, 128, 131, 142
Halvorson, Glen, 123, 131, 142, 146
Halvorson, Harold, 14
Halvorson, Henry, 4, 14
Halvorson, Herman (d. 1910), 99, 143
Halvorson, Herman (d. 1940), 87, 100, 146
Halvorson, Inga. See Isolany, Inga Halvorson
Halvorson, James, 11, 127-48
Halvorson, Kenneth, 3-4, 7, 14
Halvorson, Kim, 14
Halvorson, Michael, 3-14
Halvorson, Olaf, 5, 99-100, 127
Halvorson, Paul, 5, 18, 64-67, 83-84, 87-88, 99-100, 129, 141, 146

Halvorson, Peter C., children of, 66-67, 83, 87-90, 95, 99-100; death, 100; furlough, 87-91, 97-99; legacy of, 5, 120-21, 127-48; married, 55, 57; in South Dakota, 3-4, 88; work in Madagascar, 28, 59-87, 91-96, 120, 144-47
Halvorson, Peter J., 12, 129, 149-55
Halvorson, Phillip, 123, 131, 142
Halvorson, Ruth, 5, 37, 87-89, 95, 99-100, 127, 141
Halvorson, Solveig, 123, 131, 142
Halvorson, Sonja, 11, 127-48
Halvorson, Victor, 4-5, 66-67, 83-84, 87-88, 99-100, 141, 146
Harbeck, Alice Isolany, 100
Haslund, Mrs., 50
Herculaneum, Italy, 89
Hogstad, Rev. J. P., 60, 115-21, 141, 143
Hotel Mahavoky, 142, 144
Hull, England, 56
hymn, Malagasy, 46, 125

idol priest. See Ombiana
independence, Malagasy, 11, 86
Indian Ocean, 3, 103, 143, 145
Isolany, Alice. See Harbeck, Alice Isolany
Isolany, Arnold, 100
Isolany, Clifford, 142
Isolany, Constance, 100
Isolany, Gabriel Nilsen, 23, 27, 46, 55-57, 74, 76, 100, 120, 140-41
Isolany, Gottfred, 142
Isolany, Inga Halvorson, 57, 74, 100, 141
Isolany, Juliet. See Petersen, Juliet Isolany
Isolany, Lillian. See Froid, Lillian Isolany

Kasava (Cassava), 36, 69
Kely, Joseph, 72-73

Leborde, Jean, 40
Lellelid, Steve, 142

lemur, 37, 145, 149
leprosy, 39
Liverpool,
England, 7, 53, 55-56, 98
Loharano, mission station of, 22, 137-40; wells, 23, 137; robber raid of, 32
London Missionary Society, 111, 114, 117, 119
Ludvikson, Captain, 54
Luther, Martin, 62, 114-15
Lutheran Free Church, 125

Madagascar, climate of, 17, 103-4; environment of, 12-13, 17, 103, 144-45; history of, 8-10, 110-13; location of, 17; people of, 104-7; political instability of, 13, 110-13; president of, 14
magic. See religious beliefs, traditional
Malagasy (language), 7
Malagasy Lutheran Church, 13, 124-25, 147
malaria, 150, 154
Manafiafy station, 84
Manantantely, 75, 98
Manantenina, 84
Mananzary, 49
Marco Polo, 8
marriage (customs), 106, 119
Masinandraina, 21, 135
Mauritius, 51-55
Merina tribe (Hova), 8, 110
Minsaa family, 50-52
mission school, Ft. Dauphin. See boys' school, Ft. Dauphin
mission school, Quaker, 41
Mission Society (Norwegian), 10, 60, 92, 114-15, 119, 123-24, 132, 137
missionaries, English, 19. See also London Missionary Society
Mogadishu, 8
Morris, Ken, 14

Naples, Italy, 89
Napoleon, 54
Nilsen, Anna, 23, 25, 51-52

Nilsen, Antonette. See Halvorson, Antonette
Nilsen, Caroline, 23, 46, 53, 55-57, 74-75, 120, 141
Nilsen, Gabriel. See Isolany, Gabriel Nilsen
Nilsen, Gertrude, 23, 53-57
Nilsen, Herman Adolf (d. circa 1880), 46, 99, 140
Nilsen, Herman Adolf (d. 1958), 23, 26, 46, 55-57, 90
Nilsen, Ida, 23, 25, 55-57
Nilsen, Inga (Inge), 23, 55-57
Nilsen, Inger, 18-27, 32-34, 36, 38, 49-51, 54-57
Nilsen, Joseph, 42
Nilsen, Ommund, 23, 55-57, 90
Nilsen, Rev. Nils, death, 56; early work, 20-36, 46-47; first missionary to Madagascar, 9, 18-19, 129; furlough, 49-57; legacy, 123-25, 134-35, 140; oral history of, 138-40
Nilsen, Thomine, 23, 55-57
Nilsen-Lund, Rev., 114
Norway, return to, 26, 46, 56
Norwegian language, 7, 53
Norwegian Lutheran Church in America, 92, 104
Norwegian Mission Society. See Mission Society (Norwegian)

ody, 30, 109. See also Ombiana
Ombiana, 3, 76-78, 108-9
ordination, rite of, 70
ox meat, preparing, 44-45
oysters, 71

palace (Tananarive), 40
palanquin, 28, 50, 124, 130
Paulus, 49-56, 60, 116
Petersen, Juliet Isolany, 100
Pic St. Louis, Mt., 144-47, 154
pietism, 6
Pioneer, Washington. See Ridgefield, Washington
plants, endemic, 12; vascular, 12

Plymouth, England, 98
Pompeii, Italy, 89

Rabenja, 63-65
Radama I, 9
Radama II, 9
railroad, travel before, 35. *See also* palanquin
Rainiketamanga, 117
Rainilaiarivony, Prime Minister, 41
rain making, 30, 109
Ramahitra (Ramahatra), 39, 113
Ramananjo, 113
Ramaria, 49
Ranavalona I, 9
Ranavalona II, 19, 40, 124
Ranavalona III, 9, 40-42, 111
Randriamanga, 49
Rateaver, Eugene, 57, 92-93, 120, 143
Ravalomanana, Marc, 14
Raveljaona, 117
rebels, Malagasy, 80-87
Red Sea, 89-91
religious beliefs, traditional, 30, 76-78, 107-110. *See also Ombiana; ody*
report, evangelist school, 92-96; Ft. Dauphin Mission Station, 103-21
Reunion Island, 42
Ridgefield, Washington, 87
rock (signed by P. C. Halvorson). *See* Pic St. Louis, Mt.
Rosaas, Rev., 131

Saeterlie, Rev. M., 74, 120
school for boys (Ft. Dauphin). *See* boys' school, Ft. Dauphin
Schreuder, Bishop Hans, 18, 43, 124
Seattle, Washington, 14, 57
seminary, theological. *See* Fianarantsoa
Senegal, 86
sewing, 7, 63, 79
silkworm, 38
Sinai, South Dakota, 3, 57,
Skaar, Mr. and Mrs., 57
slave trade, 8
smallpox, 27

Sogndalen, Norway, 56
Solo, 132, 138, 149
Somalia, 8
South Africa, 55, 97, 124
St. Helena, 54
St. Olaf College, 92, 143
Stavanger, Norway, 18, 27, 55-56, 132
Stolee, Rev. M. J., 83, 85, 116
submarines, 97
Suez Canal, 89

Tamatave, 123
Tambolo (tribe), 104-7
Tananarive (Tana). *See* Antananarivo
Tandroy (tribe), 104-7
Tanosy (tribe), 104-7, 114, 118
Tanzania, 13
Taolagnaro. *See* Ft. Dauphin
Tatsimo (tribe), 104-7
Thompson, Caroline, 116
Tingwold, Anna, 42, 50, 52
Torvik, Rev. G., 84, 94
traveler's palm, 104
Trondhjem, Norway, 60, 115
Trygstad, William and Mrs., 116
tuberculosis, 32, 150
Twain, Mark, 8

Ulrack, Antonette Thorkelsdotter, 18
United Norwegian Lutheran Church in America, 104

Vesuvius, Mt., 89
vintana, 110
volcano. *See* Vesuvius

warriors, Malagasy, 29
wars, colonial, 10
wax museum (Liverpool), 55-56
witch doctor. *See Ombiana*
Women's Missionary Federation, 79
World War I, 97-98

Zan. See baobab tree

ABOUT THE
AUTHORS

Antonette Nilsen Halvorson (1870-1966) was born in Masinandraina, Madagascar, the daughter of missionary parents. She spent her childhood years watching Lutheran missionaries work with Malagasy families in the interior, and then moved to Ridgefield, Washington, in 1888 when her family returned from the mission field by way of their home country, Norway. In 1896, she married Peter C. Halvorson, a young Lutheran pastor who wanted to go to Madagascar himself as a missionary. Between 1897 and 1916, the two worked in the Ft. Dauphin area of Madagascar as missionaries, educators, and the parents of seven children. In 1916, Antonette returned with her family to Sinai, South Dakota, where she farmed with her husband and began a lengthy correspondence with friends and former colleagues in French, Norwegian, Malagasy, and English. In 1947 (at the age of 77), she finally recorded many of her stories in the book *Loharano (The Water Spring)*. Antonette Halvorson died in St. Paul, Minnesota, in 1966 at the age of 96 years.

Michael James Halvorson (1963-) is the great-grandson of Peter and Antonette Halvorson. He earned a bachelor's degree in computer science from Pacific Lutheran University in Tacoma, Washington, and master's and doctoral degrees in history from the University of Washington in Seattle. He was employed at Microsoft Corporation as a technical editor, acquisitions editor, and localization manager from 1985 to 1993. He is the author or co-author of 25 books about computer programming and computer technology, including *Microsoft Visual Basic .NET Step by Step* and *Microsoft Office XP Inside Out*. He currently works as a visiting assistant professor of history at the University of Washington, where he teaches courses in the history of early modern Europe and the Protestant Reformation.